# Rosehaugh

## A House of its Time

*James Douglas Fletcher 1857-1927. Oil painting by the Hon. John Collier. Courtesy of Lodge Rosehaugh, No 1216.*

# Rosehaugh
## A House of its Time

**Hilda Hesling, Magdalene Maclean, Kathleen MacLeman and John Mills**

Bassman Books

Published in 2016 by Bassman Books, Burnside Cottage, Newhall, Balblair, Dingwall, IV7 8LT

First published in 1996 by Avoch Heritage Association – www.avoch.org

A catalogue record for this book is available from the British Library.

ISBN 978-0-9567908-9-7

Printed by Big Sky, The Press Building, 305 The Park, Findhorn, Forres, IV36 3TE

Layout and Design: www.russellturner.org
Set in 11/13pt Palatino

*Rosehaugh, Avoch, Black Isle from a post-card by Valentine & Sons Ltd.*

# Contents

1. *Figure in bronze of the Buddha Amida seated cross-legged in an attitude of meditation with mandorla behind, Japan, late 19th century, from the collection of the late James Douglas Fletcher of Rosehaugh, Ross-shire and presented to the National Museum of Scotland (formerly the Royal Scottish Museum) by his niece, the late Mrs Shaw of Tordarroch, Newhall, Ross-shire.*

# Preface

ROSEHAUGH was a model estate. The Fletchers were not philanthropists but they were generous and progressive landowners. We read about the joy of creation underlying the outward show of Victorian and Edwardian opulence that was the due material reward of the merchant adventurer's enterprise.

The great House, the embodiment of William Flockhart's eclectic imagination, no longer stands, but the cultivated farmland and buildings, together with the harbour, are some of the enduring and noticeable testaments to their practical idealism and economy. The great bronze Buddha too has gone from the terrace by the west door where willow herb now grows. The Enlightened One is now in the Royal Scottish Museum, Edinburgh. His serene and compassionate face always impressed me as a small boy when I used to visit my great aunt at Rosehaugh every Friday. The silent gaze of the Buddha seems to say something more than the sentiment of the classical epitaph of Thomas à Kempis in the Middle Ages – "Sic transit Gloria Mundi".

In the silence of thought and study, this book illustrates the truth that in narrative history, by touching the particular, one touches the Universal. In an age of computers with standard phrases and ideas, local history, in contrast, can be the refreshing open door to an infinite world for the child and adult alike, and a most valuable inspiration in education.

In many ways, James Douglas Fletcher is a man of our own times, a pioneer who consolidated his wealth in the Highlands, destined to become a legend almost within his lifetime. This book is a work of objective research drawing upon living memory as well as copious documents. Its timely publication separates fact from fiction before memories inevitably become consigned to legend. In publishing the first edition of this book, the Avoch Heritage Association could have been called in truth the guardian of local tradition. It is to be hoped that this second edition, with small alterations by three of the four original authors, may long keep alive the cherished memory of the spirit of Rosehaugh.

JOHN SHAW OF TORDARROCH
Newhall
October 1996
November 2016

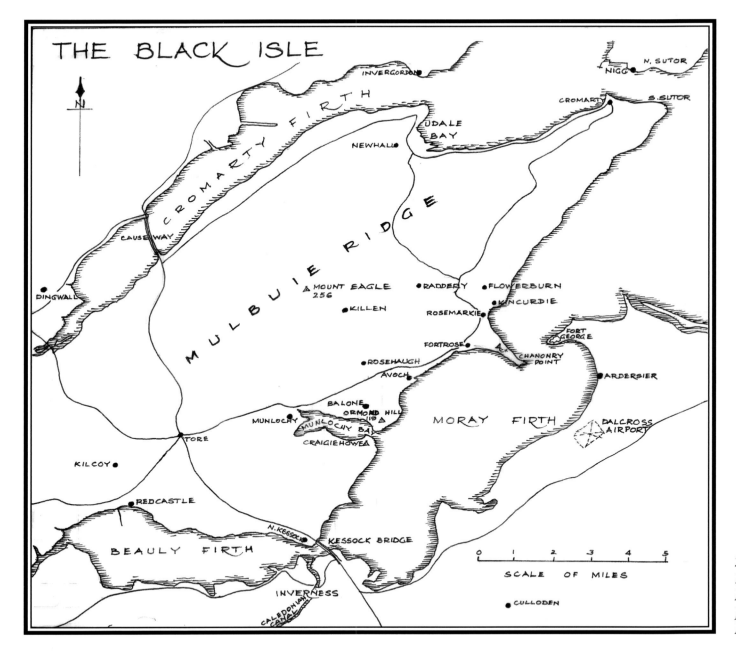

THE BLACK ISLE

N

CROMARTY FIRTH

INVERGORDON

N. SUTOR

NIGG

CROMARTY

S. SUTOR

UDALE BAY

NEWHALL

CAUSEWAY

MULBUIE RIDGE

DINGWALL

MOUNT EAGLE
256

RADDERY

FLOWERBURN

KINCURDIE

KILLEN

ROSEMARKIE

FORT GEORGE

FORTROSE

CHANONRY POINT

ROSEHAUGH

AVOCH

ARDERSIER

BALONE

ORMOND HILL
110

MORAY FIRTH

MUNLOCHY

MUNLOCHY BAY

DALCROSS AIRPORT

TORE

CRAIGIEHOWE

KILCOY

REDCASTLE

N. KESSOCK

KESSOCK BRIDGE

BEAULY FIRTH

0  1  2  3  4  5

SCALE OF MILES

INVERNESS

CALEDONIAN CANAL

CULLODEN

2. The
Black Isle.
Map by
John
Mills.

# Chapter 1: Introduction

CROSS north over the graceful span of the Kessock Bridge today and you will see the road sign announcing your arrival on the 'Black Isle'. You may well wonder how this green and fertile peninsula came by its name. Almost encircled by the thumb and forefinger of the Beauly and Cromarty Firths, it projects into the Moray Firth, twenty miles long, by a maximum of eight miles wide and consists mainly of fertile rolling farmland, with a spiny ridge of former moor called the Millbuie and rounded forested hills on either side of the bays of the eastern seaboard. To the north, the cliffs of the Sutors guard the entrance to the deep anchorages of the Cromarty Firth and at Fortrose a long promontory of land called Chanonry curls into the sea, pointing towards its twin on the south side of the Moray Firth. West of Kessock, the shallow waters of the Beauly Firth, with its extensive mudflats, sweep round past the ruins of the ancient fortress of Redcastle towards Beauly. Yet, until the 1980s, you would have had to make this now brief journey by ferry, unless you took the hour-long detour around the head of the Beauly Firth and for many centuries access to the towns and villages of the east coast of the Black Isle was almost entirely by boat. Seen from the sea, the names 'Black Isle' and its Gaelic equivalent 'Eilean Dubh' become much easier to understand: the moorland of the Millbuie and the partially wooded hills must have seemed 'dark, bleak and black' as the geologist

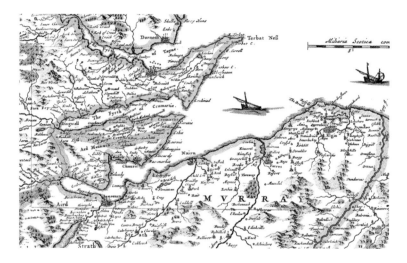

*3. Part of a map by Johannes Blaeu, Amsterdam, c1662.*

Hugh Miller called them, rising out of a grey sea, especially in winter, against the snowy slopes of the far mountains.

Favoured with a warm climate, good land and natural harbours, the Black Isle has attracted successive waves of raiders and settlers over many centuries. In times before written records, we can find evidence in stone, pottery and other artefacts of Stone, Bronze and Iron Age settlements and, best known of all, the intricately carved Rosemarkie stones bear witness to the area's Pictish

4. *Avoch from the sea. Oil painting by an unknown artist, c1880.*

inhabitants. There were settlements of the old Celtic church on the Black Isle and Rosemarkie itself is a religious centre of great antiquity. As the country emerged from the Dark Ages there are fragments of chronicles and deeds, showing the strategic importance of 'Ardmeanach' as the Black Isle was then known. In response to the incursions of Edward I of England, the Scottish Standard was raised in 1297 at Ormond Castle near Avoch, the northern stronghold of the De Moravia family, the Morays: Andrew Moray 'of Bothwell and Avoch', Regent of Scotland, died here in 1338.

Connections between the two sides of the Moray Firth have always been close and there are many links of kinship and land ownership. The Bishop of Ross, with an ecclesiastical eye for a fertile spot, built his cathedral at 'Chanonry', now Fortrose, which later provided a stopping place on James IV's 'Royal Route' of pilgrimage, from Moray, with its cathedral at Elgin, to the shrine of St Duthac at Tain.

An unnamed Chronicler of 1711 described the Black Isle thus:

*'That part of Rosse next to the Murray Firth, tho' pretty mountainous, is very fruitful in corn towards the Shoar and on the Banks of the Rivers. Fruit trees and Herbs are much better here than could be expected from the Climate. The Peninsula which lies between the Bays of Cromarty and Murray is called Ardmeanach upon the Shoar of which stands the Town call'd the Chanrie of Rosse, formerly a Bishop's See. It is pleasantly situated in a valley betwixt pleasant and fruitful Hills.'* [1]

During the century that followed, the coastal communities flourished. In the late 18th and early 19th centuries, Cromarty was the centre of a thriving merchant trade across the North Sea and its many fine old buildings bear witness today to its prosperous past. West of Fortrose lies the fishing village of Avoch, which of all the places on the Black Isle has maintained its identity intact. The fishing people here formed a tight knit community, with their own dialect form of English, their own family groups, their own customs and superstitions. No-one knows for sure where they came from: yet everyone agrees that they must have been sea-borne incomers, possibly from Cornwall, or from Holland or France.

The description by the local minister in the Old Statistical Account (1793) shows the spectacular growth of the fishing industry in Avoch at this time. The village consisted of three small communities: Seatown, Kirktown and Milltown:

*'About the end of the last century, there was only one fishing boat here - the village of Seatown which contains at present 93 families has been mostly, if not entirely, built since that period and the fishermen there are now the equal to any in the north of Scotland for hardiness, skill and industry, though their distance from the main ocean subjects them to many inconveniences.'* [2]

The men and women of the village were:

*'mostly of a middle size, strong and healthy and capable of enduring a good deal of fatigue and labour.'* [3]

Their cottages clustered close to the shore, in streets built gable-end to the sea and named after the sons and womenfolk of the MacKenzie lairds. A mile inland stood Rosehaugh House, seat of the MacKenzies of Scatwell. In 1864 the house was bought by James Fletcher, originally from Moray, whose parents had married in Elgin two years after the Minister's account of Avoch was published.

This book tells the story of Rosehaugh House and its owners.

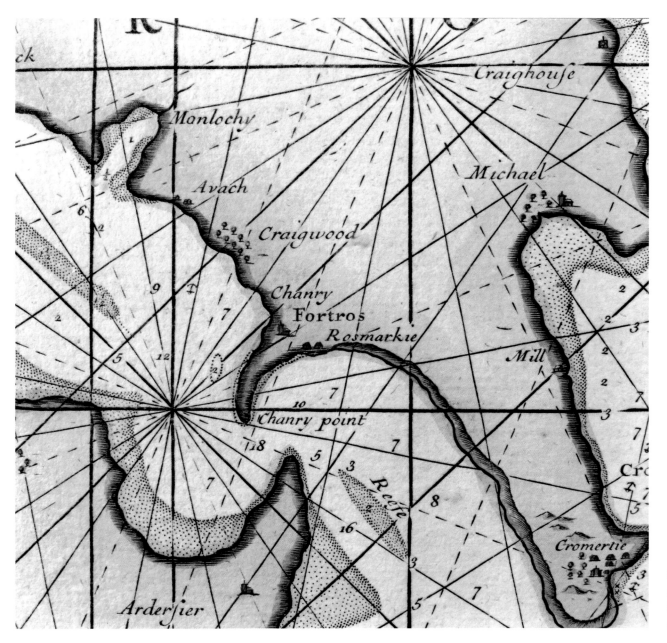

Craighouse

Monlochy

Michael

Avach

Craigwood

Chanry
Fortros
Rosmarkie

Mill

Chanry point

Reese

Cromertie

Ardersier

Cr

5. *Part of a sea-chart by Captain Grenville Collins, c1695.*

4

# Chapter 2: The MacKenzies

'THE lands of Pittanochtie, called the lands of Rosehaugh' which James Fletcher bought in 1864 represented the final sale of the once extensive estates of Sir James John Randall MacKenzie, sixth Baronet of Scatwell. The canny lawyers were always meticulous in using the two names for the estate: Pittanochtie, the original one, used since mediaeval times, and Rosehaugh, the much more recent one, given by a new owner in the 17th century to a patchwork of lands adjoining. This patchwork of lands did not at first include the mediaeval Pittanochtie, but the name 'Rosehaugh' was later used for the mansion house and estate lands of Pittanochtie.

These lands are mentioned as early as the 14th century, and the early - and many of the later! - scribes have a dozen variations on the spelling, all referring to the fertile south facing slopes shown as the 'Hills of Pittanicty' on Roy's Military Map of c1750 (see illustration 6). During the 14th century, the Morays, and then the Douglases, both powerful families involved in the turbulent dynastic struggles of the times, held sway here and later these lands were forfeit to the Crown and thence, in the 16th century, to the Bishop of Ross.

In the late 1660s, the lands of Pittanochtie were acquired by grant by Sir George MacKenzie, known to history, uncharitably perhaps, as the 'Bloody MacKenzie' for his persecution of religious dissenters in the name of the Crown. He was the son of Simon MacKenzie of Lochslin Castle, near Tain, brother of the Earl of Seaforth, head of the MacKenzies. These MacKenzie chiefs were Lords of Kintail in the west and Brahan in the east, and another branch were Earls of Cromartie. They founded large families, who, as often as not, married MacKenzie cousins and between them they held large portions of the eastern seaboard of Ross in a close woven web of kinship and marriage alliances and produced several men prominent in the political, legal and scholastic circles of 17th and 18th century Scotland. George MacKenzie (see illustration 7) was one of the most outstanding. He was born in Dundee in 1636 and seems to have been a young man of exceptional gifts. He studied at Aberdeen and St Andrews Universities, and in Bourges, central France. He was admitted to the Scottish Bar in 1656 and had a brilliant legal career, becoming Lord Advocate in 1677. His principal residence was near Edinburgh at Shank in East Lothian. In the late 1660s he began to acquire various areas of land on the Black Isle, some by purchase, some by grant from the Church and Crown, no doubt as a reward for his legal services. This gave him the necessary residency qualification to stand for Parliament and, as his father had been before him, he was elected Member for Ross in 1669.

He now owned mill lands at Rosemarkie and Avoch, the lands of Pittanochtie and Arkendeith, portions of land at Balmungie and Wester Raddery, some other small areas and the coastal strip and the woods known as the Craig Woods between Avoch and Fortrose. He was knighted in 1674 and took the title 'Sir George MacKenzie of Rosehaugh'. The name 'Rosehaugh' seems to have been given by Sir George to some of his patchwork of lands in the area, though not, at this time, to Pittanochtie.

Over a century later the writer of the Old Statistical Account in 1793 describes the strip of land between Avoch and Fortrose thus:

*'This wood marks part of the old estate of Rosehaugh, which belonged to the late celebrated Sir George MacKenzie, King's Advocate. The property is said to be so named from a small haugh (stream) contiguous to the bank, where a great many sweetbriars and wild roses used to grow...it is said that Sir George MacKenzie was so fond of this walk, and of that on Chanonry Point...that he used to call it rudeness and want of taste in any of his friends to ride on horseback along them.'* [4]

This romantic notion that the name came from the wild roses is attractive, but perhaps slightly fanciful and there may be a simpler one. Many names in this area start with 'ros', being a form of the Gaelic for promontory, and 'haugh' means shallow waters, a watering-place or a field by a stream, as in the name of Avoch, pronounced 'och'. It may therefore be an anglicised form of 'ros-haugh', and the fact that the name Rosehaugh appears as a farm name in a rent book of the MacKenzies backs up this more prosaic explanation. Be that as it may, George MacKenzie clearly found his lands in Ross a source of refreshment after the legal and political hothouse of Edinburgh. He built a small L-shaped house on the lands of Pittanochtie, near the farm called Rosehaugh Mains on the rent-book of 1762.

In 1688, the year of the Glorious Bloodless Revolution,

*6. Roy's Military Map c1750. Courtesy of the British Library.*

George MacKenzie had been one of a small minority opposing the accession of William of Orange. As a consequence he felt it prudent to retire from public life and left Edinburgh. Just before his departure he formally opened the Advocates' Library in Edinburgh, later the National Library, which he had instituted and this alone would ensure him a place in Scottish history. The same year he sold the lands of Pittanochtie to his cousin. George went to Oxford, to pursue literary studies and died on a visit to London, two years later. He left his other Ross-shire lands, the amalgamation of smaller properties known collectively as Rosehaugh to his family, and in 1739 his great grandson, the Right Honourable James Stewart MacKenzie, who was to become Lord Privy Seal of Scotland, succeeded to this estate of Rosehaugh. In 1752 he sold it to George Ross of Pitkeerie, and kept only the empty title and some rights of superiority.

Meantime, Kenneth MacKenzie, who had bought Pittanochtie from Sir George MacKenzie, had married a MacKenzie heiress, Lilias MacKenzie of Findon, in 1696. This extended his estates considerably: he now owned Pittanochtie and Findon and a few years later succeeded to the family lands of Scatwell, further west on the River Conon and Lochluichart. He was created first Baronet of Scatwell in 1703.

In 1711 a Chronicler lists as one of the principal 'Seats of Rosse' that of 'Pittonarthy', belonging to the 'MacKenzie of Scatwel'. In fact, during most of the 18th century the family seems to have lived at Findon, on the north side of the Black Isle, where their house had, in Latin, over the door, the touching inscription 'nothing certain, save my own house'. Sir Kenneth MacKenzie's son, Roderick, married Janet Grant of the family of Seafield and letters of hers, dated from Rosehaugh, are to be found in the British Library. Perhaps, even then, the family called the 'old house' of George MacKenzie by this name of Rosehaugh. What is certain is that Roderick MacKenzie's grandson and namesake built a new mansion in the 1790s and called it Rosehaugh House. The Reverend James Smith, Minister of Avoch, describes it in the Old Statistical Account as follows:

*'His seat of Rosehaugh-House stands on a beautiful bank, about a mile and a half from the sea, on the north side of the southern vale. It is a modern edifice, substantially built and commodious; and cost between 3000L-4000L sterling.'* [5]

The site of this house was further inland and slightly further uphill from the site of the 'Bloody' MacKenzie's one. Unfortunately no drawings or prints of it are extant, but a later family member, not sharing the enthusiasm of the minister, writes of it being 'a plain square white house of no great size'. The ground plan on an 1844 garden design (see illustration 77) shows just this outline, with one bay window to the east and another to the western side.

The MacKenzie family moved out of Findon now and settled at Rosehaugh. Sir Roderick, the builder of the mansion, had two sons. They both seem to have been a trial to him: but in particular, the younger, James Wemyss, on account of his extravagance and youthful dalliance with a native lady in the West Indies, became estranged from his father. After his return to Scotland, he married another MacKenzie heiress, Henrietta of Suddie, neighbouring Rosehaugh to the west. Shortly afterwards, in 1810, the death occurred of Lewis, his elder brother and heir to the estates. The Minister of Avoch records that old Sir Roderick, beside himself with grief,

*'ordered out his great yellow chariot and drove over to call on the newly married pair at Suddie House, to the great admiration of the whole countryside, for all knew he had not been on speaking terms with either of his sons.'* [6]

By the following year, Sir Roderick was dead, and James Wemyss was installed as fifth Baronet at Rosehaugh. James and his beloved 'Henny' settled down most contentedly and James became an exemplary laird, taking a great interest in farming and local affairs. In 1812, after he had taken over, he had made a fine new range of farm buildings. He became Member of Parliament for the county of Ross in 1824 and later Lord Lieutenant of the county.

In 1839 he describes his daily round thus:

*7. Sir George MacKenzie of Rosehaugh – 1636-1691, after an oil painting by Sir Godfrey Kneller. Courtesy of the Scottish National Portrait Gallery.*

*'I cannot walk much but I drive about in my gig all around my property which is a great matter to me, seeing many improvements going on in my Mains and the tenants improving also, as they are bound to do in their new leases, but they require great looking after.'* [7]

In 1840 the dearly loved Henrietta died and Sir James's health went into an immediate decline. He died in March 1843 and was succeeded by his only son, James John Randall MacKenzie, born in 1814 and educated at Westminster and Trinity College, Cambridge. He had married, in 1838, Lady Anne Wentworth, daughter of Earl Fitzwilliam and there was great family rejoicing at this grand alliance, at the prospect of new money as much as that of an heir. Already in 1839, there was a report that the shooting lodge at Kinlochluichart had been extended as 'Lady Anne is so much delighted with the place' and once James John Randall was in charge at Rosehaugh, there was to be no stopping him.

He carried on with planned extensions to the Mains Farm, stables, lodges and keepers' cottages at Scatwell itself and with new lodges and cottages at Rosehaugh. Lady Anne's father was at first generous in support of his extravagant son-in-law, but all thoughts of prudence rapidly went to the winds with extensions to the house and a new garden. Sir James and Lady Anne had no children and the next to inherit under the terms of the entail executed by Sir Roderick the Fourth Baronet were the children of the two brothers of Sir Roderick. As the estate was already heavily burdened, the consent of these cousins had to be forthcoming before any further borrowing could be undertaken. This was eventually obtained, but Sir James tried the family's patience to the limits with endless litigation, all the while living well beyond his means and borrowing from one lender to repay another. He was not without disinterested advice: only five years after he inherited, his kindly old neighbour, Duncan

Davidson of Tulloch Castle, Dingwall, was writing to him:

*'My dear Sir James: As I am a much older man than you, and as I feel a real and sincere friendship for you I hope you will not take amiss what I am going to write. I know that you, at present, like myself, have some embarrassments of a pecuniary nature. Very few indeed are now exempt who have exercised as much hospitality as you have. Lovat, Col Baillie, Mrs Stewart MacKenzie, myself and others have been obliged to pull up, reduce establishments, let shootings... You can have every comfort which this country can afford, with a house to keep up, inclusive of sufficient shooting for yourself and a few friends, for from £1500-1600 a year.'*

'Old Tulloch', as he was affectionately known, goes on to 'prove' this and his calculations give a fascinating insight into the costs of running a large house and estate at this time:

*'living, including every expense of the house*

| | |
|---|---:|
| *at £60 per month, with coals, wine, groceries etc.* | £720 |
| *allow for garden* | £100 |
| *allow for game* | £100 |
| *allow for servants, including butler, page, coachman, helper, house-keeper, cook, lady's maid, house-maid, two laundry-maids, under house-maid* | £266 |
| *say, two ponies, including saddlery* | £100 |
| *taxes about* | £70 |
| | £1356 |
| *for clothes and sundries* | £244 |
| | £1600 |

*To show you how much your neighbours feel the pressure of the times, Lovat has let his deer forest, and is ploughing up the park to near the doors; has reduced his establishment in every way. Mrs Stewart MacKenzie (at Brahan) has reduced hers to the lowest point. Col Baillie (Redcastle) has sent all his men from the garden but one and some lads - one keeper only is retained and all the improvements stopp'd... I write to remove any unpleasant feeling which you might entertain by coming to reside with a smaller establishment than you have been accustomed to...'* [8]

Tulloch might as well have saved himself the trouble: 'reducing' was not on Sir James's agenda. His reply to Old Tulloch's letter was the formal minimum required by courtesy. He continued to flounder ever deeper into debt. He had raised large sums of money on the security of the 'lands of Pittanochtie' and during the late 1850s most of the rest of his properties were sold to repay these loans. It was never going to be enough. By 1862 the sixth Baronet of Scatwell was bankrupt. Two years later the sale of his last piece of negotiable property was made to James Fletcher and, estranged from his family, insolvent, and supported only by the faithful Lady Anne, he was obliged to leave not just Rosehaugh, but Great Britain. He went to France and died at Versailles in 1884.

James Fletcher, the new laird of Rosehaugh - the old name of Pittanochtie was now abandoned for ever - was very nearly the exact contemporary of James John Randall MacKenzie. He was seven years older and outlived him by just one year - but his origins, his career and his fortunes could hardly have been more different.

# Jack
## Family Tree

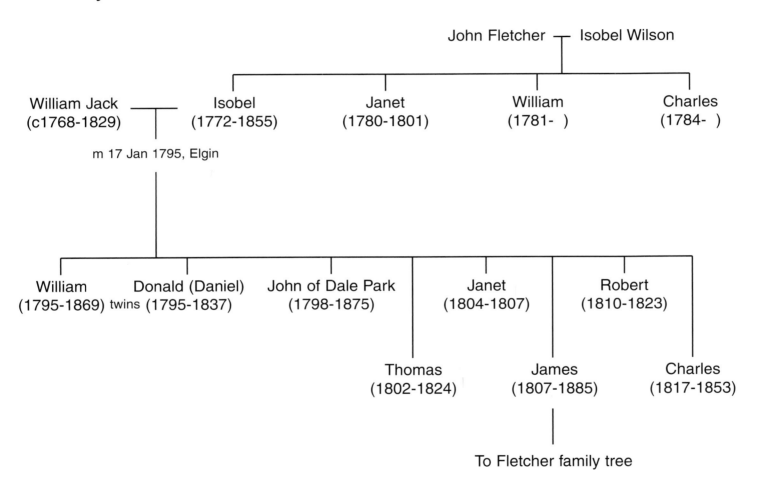

John Fletcher — Isobel Wilson

William Jack — Isobel (1772-1855)   Janet (1780-1801)   William (1781- )   Charles (1784- )
(c1768-1829)

m 17 Jan 1795, Elgin

William (1795-1869) twins   Donald (Daniel) (1795-1837)   John of Dale Park (1798-1875)   Janet (1804-1807)   Robert (1810-1823)

Thomas (1802-1824)   James (1807-1885)   Charles (1817-1853)

To Fletcher family tree

*8. Family tree of the Jacks.*

# Chapter 3: The Jacks

JAMES Jack, later to become Fletcher, was born in Elgin, Morayshire, the fifth son of William Jack and Isobel Fletcher. William Jack was born in approximately 1768 and it is said that he originated from the fishing village of Avoch, but the relevant church records are missing, and since record keeping in the 1700s was not always accurate, his birth place is not certain. The Fletcher family of Rosehaugh, however, have always accepted that their roots lay in Avoch.

Isobel Fletcher was the daughter of Isobel Wilson and John Fletcher who was a farm overseer at the Shank of Barriewas, Marnoch in Banffshire. Their daughter, Isobel, was born there on 3 November, 1772, and the births of her two brothers, William and Charles, are recorded in 1781 and 1784 respectively. Although there are no registered births of any sisters, the name Janet, appears on the Jack plaque in Elgin Cathedral as having died in 1801, aged 21.

William Jack was a nailer, a skilled occupation similar to that of a blacksmith, and he practised his trade in premises on Charles Close in Elgin. William and Isobel married on 17 January 1795, in the Parish Church of Elgin 'before a competent number of witnesses'. The couple had seven sons and one daughter, Janet, who did not survive to adulthood. The first born were twin sons, William and Donald, and of the five other sons, we are particularly interested in John, born 28 August 1798, James, born 22 August 1807 and Charles, born 1 June 1817.

All the sons attended Elgin Academy, which must have been quite an undertaking for their father at that time. They received what the Elgin Courier called an 'excellent education', and the boys 'had good abilities, were attentive to their studies and became excellent scholars'. No further education is recorded for them, but the twins, William and Donald, are mentioned as merchants, grocers and stoneware dealers. Three of the boys showed promising business acumen, and John, James and eventually Charles, left Elgin to apply their skills in Liverpool.

Liverpool was the mercantile centre, not only of Great Britain, but also of the whole Empire, importing raw materials and exporting finished goods. It was the port through which the growing factories of the North of England were supplied, particularly with cotton and wool, and many men made their fortune there. John and James founded a trading house in Liverpool called Jack Brothers, with respectable office premises at 3 Rumford Place, close to the Exchange Buildings, now the Town Hall.

The commodity in which they became involved was not a conventional one, but the wool of the alpaca which is long and silken in texture. The alpaca is one of the camel family, akin to the llama, and these animals live on the slopes of the Andes in South America at heights of between 4000 and 5000 metres. In 1841, the Highland

9. *James Jack, later Fletcher.*

10. *Frederica Mary Jack, later Fletcher, née Stephen.*

Agricultural Society offered a medal for the first pair of alpacas to be born and bred in Scotland, but all attempts failed.

The wool of the alpaca was used to produce a lustrous cloth, which in the 1830s was fashionable and in great demand for ladies' dress goods. Peru was the only source of supply and Arequipa, in the south, regional capital of the Altiplano, the High Plain, was the main centre of the trade. The South American Indians in the Andes transported the wool by llama to the area around Lake Titicaca where it was sold to the small number of merchants based in Arequipa. In 1834, the quantity of alpaca wool exported from Peru was 5700 lbs, but by 1839 this had increased to 1,325,000 lbs and it remained in great demand for years to come.

John Jack remained in Liverpool controlling the sales of their alpaca cargo which was mainly sold to the West Riding worsted industry, but he also accepted commissions from other trades for the transporting of goods. At the same time, James went to Arequipa to build up trade. Peru was not an ideal place to be, being prone to revolutions, earthquakes and 'fearful epidemics'. As Eric Sigsworth says in his book *Black Dyke Mills*, 'conditions under which the alpaca flourished were primitive and the trade required special abilities'.

While James was in Peru, Charles, the youngest brother, moved from Elgin to join the business in Liverpool. In 1838, John, having adopted John Charles as his Christian names, married Elizabeth Church and they set up home in Liverpool at 3 Bedford Street South near Abercromby Square.

In 1845, James returned home to Britain. His father had died in 1829 at the age of 61 and the elder twin brother, Donald, had died in 1837 aged 41, but his mother, now aged 73, grandmother and the other twin, William, were still living in Elgin. During his visit to Elgin in 1846, James donated a number of items brought back from Peru, to the Elgin Museum: a case of 12 Peruvian birds, two dressed figures, six specimens of gold, two earthenware dishes, two carved nut shells, two bows and 22 arrows and the mummified figure of a girl. Of these items donated, only three remain, the earthenware dishes and the mummified figure, dated at over 2000 years old. Records in Elgin Museum archives state that the body was taken from a cave on an islet of Lake Titicaca and had probably been mummified by baking in a low heat with herbs. Her loss meant a great deal to the local Indians, and it is said that 'their suspicions of an Englishman in this matter, caused him to flee the country.'

In 1847, a monetary crisis made it extremely difficult to borrow money from the Bank of England. This made it impossible for many merchants to commit themselves to new contracts. Besides alpaca, there was also an established trade in Peru in guano, bird droppings high in phosphorus and important for use as a fertiliser. This was collected from the islands off the coast of Peru. In early 1847, the Peruvian government decided to renew all existing contracts for guano, asking for proof of financial backing. James Jack was not in Peru at that time, but returned quickly to Lima in January 1848 with drawing rights of £200,000, an enormous sum in those days. Unfortunately, he was 'much chagrined at finding the door closed' as all the contracts had been allocated to his great rival Gibbs & Co.

However the wool trade continued to flourish, and there is evidence that the brothers traded in llama and vicuna wool too. There is correspondence in the woollen mill in Elgin, showing that they bought bales of these fine wools from Jack Brothers in Liverpool. The raw material made the vast journey half-way across the world – this was before the Panama Canal was built – and Johnston & Co. had the idea of making ponchos and sending these all the way back again. The venture, as may be imagined, was not a tremendous financial success. The director of the mill wrote to James Jack, 'Your friends in Arequipa were singularly unfortunate in their recommendations…' He lost £20 on his 54 ponchos.

James returned home again in 1849 leaving Charles, the youngest brother, to manage affairs in Arequipa. An assistant, William Ricketts was sent to join him in 1852 but shortly after Ricketts' arrival, Charles died in April 1853 at the age of 35 and was buried in Arequipa. James was later to say that Charles was always 'the ablest of the three'. William Ricketts continued for many years as manager for the firm, later became a partner in Stafford & Co. and established his family and descendants as important members of the Anglo-Peruvian community in Arequipa into the 1970s.

Of the four firms controlling the trade in 1850, Jack Brothers of Liverpool and Gibbs & Co. of London were the most important. The Jack Brothers' interest in the Peruvian wool market continued for many years, although later in the century, political upheaval in Peru and changing fashions meant a decline in the trade. By then, however, their large fortunes had been invested in business enterprises in many parts of the world.

By 1851, Gore's Merchants' Directory shows the Jack Brothers had moved their premises to 10 Rumford Place in Liverpool. Meanwhile in 1850 James, now aged 43, bought the house, garden, stabling, outbuildings and land of Woolton Hill House at Woolton on the Hill, a suburb of Liverpool. This was bought from Mr James MacGregor for the sum of £4250 and had an area measuring three acres, three roods and ten perches.

Two years later, on 20 July 1852, James and Frederica Mary Stephen were married at St George's, Hanover Square, London, by the Bishop of Moray and Ross, Primus Eden (see illustrations 9, 10). Frederica was the widow of Lieutenant Alexander Macleod Hay of the 58th regiment who had died in 1849, leaving her with a baby daughter Mary, born in New Zealand. The Stephen fami-

11. Mrs Frederica Mary Fletcher, formerly Jack.

ly had settled in Melbourne, Australia, several years before Frederica's first marriage.

This family produced some distinguished members including Frederica's uncle, Sir Alfred Stephen, Chief Justice of New South Wales and Sir Leslie Stephen, founder of the National Dictionary of Biography and father of Virginia Woolf.

In the same year as James married, John, now aged 55 years, bought the Georgian mansion house Dale Park, near Arundel in Sussex, together with several thousand acres of land. John, his wife Elizabeth and family eventually resulting in two sons and five daughters, went to live there and subsequently John gradually withdrew from the business. Clearly John was well respected in Sussex, becoming Justice of the Peace, Deputy Lieutenant of the county, and in 1863 High Sheriff of Sussex. His son Charles John inherited Dale Park on his death and, in 1894, he too became High Sheriff. In turn, Charles's son, Alan Francis, inherited the property. He served in World War One, being on the staff of Field Marshall Haig and was highly decorated. In the 1930s he sold Dale Park, which was eventually demolished.

It is known that both John and James changed their surname from Jack to Fletcher in October, 1855. Their mother had died earlier that same year and on 12 October 1855 the following notice appeared in the *London Gazette*:

*'The Queen has been pleased to give and grant unto James Jack, of Woolton Hill, Liverpool, in this county of Lancaster, Esquire, Her royal licence and authority, that he and his issue may (in compliance with a wish expressed in the last will and testament of his mother, Isobel, daughter of John Fletcher of Forres, in North Britain, and widow and relict of William Jack, of Elgin, in North Britain, deceased) hence-forth assume the surname of Fletcher, instead of that of Jack:*

*And also to command that the said royal concession and declaration be recorded in Her Majesty's College of Arms.'* [9]

The reason for this wish is unknown.

By 1859, James and Frederica were the parents of four sons and one daughter. These were in order of age, Alfred Nevett, Edward Stephen, Constance Maud, James Douglas and Fitzroy Charles. In the years that followed Fitzroy's birth, Frederica's health was giving cause for concern and she died before the age of 40, possibly of consumption. At this time, James's legal representative in the north, William Grigor, who was based in Elgin, was looking for suitable property for him. When the Rosehaugh Estate became available, this was considered carefully and in 1864 James started negotiations, finally buying the estate in 1865 from James John Randall MacKenzie of Scatwell for the sum of £145,000.

# Fletcher

## Family Tree

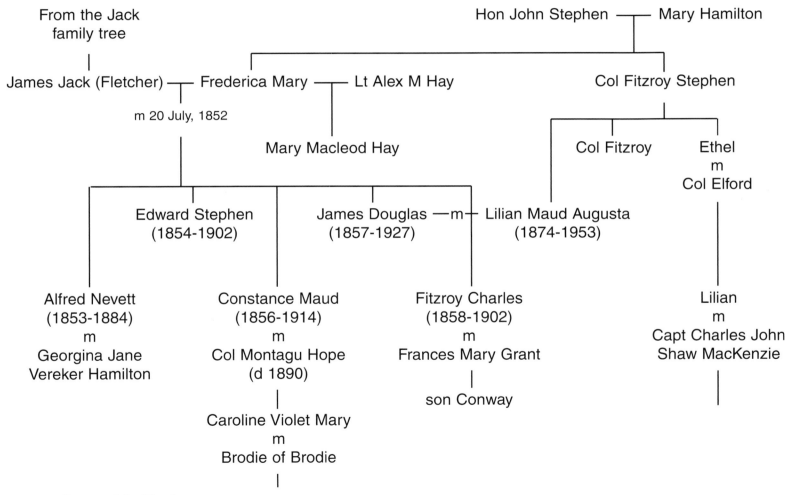

From the Jack family tree

James Jack (Fletcher) — Frederica Mary — Lt Alex M Hay

m 20 July, 1852

Mary Macleod Hay

Hon John Stephen — Mary Hamilton

Col Fitzroy Stephen

Col Fitzroy

Ethel
m
Col Elford

Edward Stephen (1854-1902)

James Douglas —m— Lilian Maud Augusta (1857-1927)        (1874-1953)

Alfred Nevett (1853-1884)
m
Georgina Jane Vereker Hamilton

Constance Maud (1856-1914)
m
Col Montagu Hope (d 1890)

Caroline Violet Mary
m
Brodie of Brodie

Fitzroy Charles (1858-1902)
m
Frances Mary Grant

son Conway

Lilian
m
Capt Charles John Shaw MacKenzie

*12. Family tree of the Fletchers.*

# Chapter 4: The Fletchers

AS the years advanced, James's business acumen did not diminish with age, but, on the contrary, gained momentum. Not only did he remain in control of his world-wide merchant business in Liverpool, ever widening its commercial interests, but he also embarked on a series of land acquisitions in the Black Isle and in Forfarshire.

In 1865 Rosehaugh Estate extended to 6,400 acres and to this was added: Aythe (Eathie), Craighead, Learnie, Easter and Wester Muirhead bought from Baillie of Dochfour in 1866; Bennagefield (Bennetsfield) bought from Sir James Matheson of Achany in 1867; land at Millbuy (Millbuie) bought from Major Nicolson of Hawkhill in 1869; Millbuy Brae; Cromarty bought from Roderick MacKenzie of Flowerburn in 1871; part of Avoch and Knockmuir (also called Wester Farneise) bought from Major General Kirkland of Kent in 1872; Mount Pleasant bought from Mrs Helen MacDonald-Hobhouse and the Wester Glebe of Avoch bought from the Presbytery of Chanonry, both in 1877; lands and estate of Ardmeanach bought from the Trustees of the late Colin MacKenzie of Newhall in 1879; the old Commonty Lands of Millbuy bought from Colin M. Milne Millar of Kincurdy in 1883 – resulting in a total of 10,600 acres.

On taking over the ownership, James immediately embarked upon schemes of reclamation and improvements on a massive and expensive scale, attempting and succeeding where no-one would have believed possible. The most ambitious of these ventures was the draining of Loch Scadden, situated above Avoch, between Limekilns and Craiglands and covering almost six acres. The excavation of a 15 feet deep canal through the Loch with numerous branch drains on either side successfully drained the area, thereafter leaving the soil to produce the richest of crops. Of 887 acres of moor and heath, 600 acres were reclaimed for cultivation in four years with mossy areas drained to a depth of 10 feet; stones being laid in main drains and tiles from the Morayshire Tileworks in branch drains. A gross total of 3300 acres of waste and improvable land was reclaimed, enclosed, drained or planted including the construction of 15 miles of wire fencing and 15 miles of dykes, but not including the repairs to existing cultivated acreages.

Such improvements of the land led to the necessity for improvements to, and the construction of, farm buildings and it was for that reason that James advanced money on interest to tenants, now on 19 year leases. Little escaped the attention of James - old roads were repaired; new ones constructed; farm cottages suitable for married accommodation were built; farms rearranged to a more economically viable size, averaging 100-150 acres – in all matters he must have relied heavily on Grigor & Young, Solicitors, Elgin, who managed the estate initially, followed by factors Beattie, Robert Black and, from 1878, John Henderson.

13. *Henrietta Bridge, Avoch. Gas lighting and water pump.*

Rosehaugh Mains which then extended to 500 acres was, along with Muirhead, retained under the Laird's control, the Mains being managed by Mr Lawson, a very able and competent man. With careful selection of bulls, regardless of expense, the home farm's cross Shorthorn bullocks became highly regarded all over the North and the further introduction of Shorthorn cows was the beginning of a scheme to provide pure bred bulls for the use of tenants.

A business man for the greater part of his life, James's improvements were mainly planned with long-term benefits in mind. The village of Avoch had always been divided between the two estates, Avoch and Rosehaugh, resulting in neither landowner taking responsibility for the dreadful living conditions of the people, who were desperately poor. In a hundred years no organised improvements had been executed and the village was left without the most basic of facilities. Under the sole ownership of James, sanitary arrangements were improved and a street scavenger employed from 1881. Street water pumps were installed and gas street lighting was switched on in 1885 amidst great celebrations (see illustration 13). Seven years prior to this James had sold most of the village to the occupiers while retaining the feus.

There were few aspects of life in the area in which James did not become involved. The Avoch Parish Church had been badly damaged by fire, and on its reconstruction in 1870, James donated a stained glass window.

Following the Disruption of the Church in 1843 the Free Church approached Sir James John Randall MacKenzie of Rosehaugh requesting a church site but, being a staunch opponent of the Disruption, he refused. Matheson of Bennetsfield, however, with an impish humour, provided a site on the top of the hill located in such a spot that Sir James could not fail to see it every morning from his windows at Rosehaugh. The location was somewhat remote and a new site was agreed with James Fletcher, the land rent to be 1/- with James donating £500 towards building costs and a proviso that he engage the architect. Alexander Ross of Inverness designed the new Free Church which opened free of debt in 1873. With the Union of the Churches in 1900, it became the United Free Church, later still the Village Hall and is now the private residence 'Tower House' situated above and to the west of the village football pitch (see illustration 14).

Due to his life-long regard for the importance of education, James remedied the lack of such provision in Killen by having a substantial school and schoolhouse built at a cost exceeding £700 and these buildings were bought from him by the later established School Board in 1874 with the proviso that they remain in trust. The payment of £3 feu duty was always returned by James. Barely two months before his death, James was invited to lay the foundation stone of the new buildings at Elgin Academy, and, on so doing, he donated £500 towards the building fund.

At the age of 60 in 1867, James, now a widower, was faced with the task of bringing up a young family of five, their ages ranging from nine to 14. His sons' education was a priority and Eton was his choice, with Alfred being the first to attend in 1867, followed at intervals by James Douglas and Fitzroy Charles. Edward Stephen, the second son, required special care and attention throughout his life and as a result did not attend Eton with his brothers.

James believed in achieving the best possible results that money could buy and his daughter's wedding was the happy occasion and opportunity for him to prove it, the nuptials taking place in Inverness Cathedral at 11.30am on 2 November 1876 with 120 guests in attendance.

Constance Maud's gown was of white satin trimmed with Brussels lace, orange blossom and syringa, and she was accompanied by eight bridesmaids dressed in ecru

14. *The Free Church, later the United Free Church, by Alexander Ross, architect, Inverness, 1873.*

Indian muslin edged with ruby velvet and Gainsborough hats trimmed to match. Captain Montagu Hope of Luffness, serving in the Gordon Highlanders, was the groom, with his brother in attendance as best man. The Caledonian Hotel was the venue for the wedding breakfast with the function rooms and corridors appropriately decorated in crimson and tartan.

The wedding cake was of such dimensions that it warranted a separate mention in the newspapers of the time, weighing 406 lbs without ornaments, rising five tiers to a height of six feet from a base of 14 feet in circumference and decorated with white satin banners carrying monograms and mottoes, floral sprigs and vases, surmounted by a bouquet of orange blossom, camellias, lily of the valley and silver ferns with a centre piece in the style of the fountain at the Louvre. This masterpiece was achieved by Mr MacDonald of the Peacock, Inverness, a man whose reputation for such cakes had already spread beyond the Highlands.

Many beautiful and expensive gifts were presented to the bride including a diamond and pearl necklace accompanied by a Moroccan leather travelling bag with silver clasps from her father; an aquamarine and pearl necklace with earrings from Alfred; a breakfast service of Danish china from James Douglas and a framed Dresden painting on porcelain from Fitzroy Charles.

The guest list was equally impressive, not only including friends and relations who had travelled from all parts of Britain, but also a large and distinguished gathering of Highland gentry and dignitaries – Sir Kenneth and Lady MacKenzie of Gairloch, Lord and Lady MacDonald of the Isles and Colonel and Mrs Ross of Cromarty, to name but a few. Many local business people attended including Provost Grant of Fortrose and also the Reverend Gibson of Avoch. Celebrations continued into the evening with a dinner and ball held at Rosehaugh for the tenants and neighbours, and bonfires lit up the sky all over the estate.

Sadly such impressive nuptials did not guarantee a long and happy married life, and though the marriage was blessed with the birth of a child, Caroline Violet Mary, in September 1878, it was dissolved by Colonel Hope in 1882. He maintained contact with the Fletcher family and Caroline Violet enjoyed happy times at Rosehaugh from childhood to her own marriage.

Alfred Nevett, James Fletcher's eldest son, caused his father constant concern, never settling to an occupation despite his Eton schooling, merely having the capacity to spend money and to keep unacceptable company, both to a considerable extent. Alfred further irritated his father by entering into a series of marriage contracts with the representatives of Georgina Jane Vereker Hamilton of Melbourne, without consulting his father, yet binding him to honour the said contracts in certain circumstances. The marriage took place 'on or about the 25th November 1880' and the couple returned to Britain to take up residence at Woolton Hill House, Liverpool, where they lived for three years until concern for Alfred's health prompted them to leave for warmer climes before the onset of the 1884 winter. However Alfred died at Folkestone and his remains were brought to Avoch and interred in the family vault on 5 October.

Of James's five children James Douglas displayed the greatest potential, achieving reasonable success at Eton during the years 1871 to 1876 under the guidance of William Wayte, and transferring to Balliol College, Oxford, where he read Law and gained a third-class degree in Jurisprudence in 1880. Meanwhile, Fitzroy Charles had remained barely three years at Eton, furthering his education instead by travelling in Germany and France, whence he returned at the age of 20 to a commission in the Royal Scots Greys, a distinguished cavalry regiment. Here Fitzroy discovered his great affinity with horses and became a very skilled horseman. His military career ended five years later when he left the service with

15. *Rosehaugh House c1880, with extensions by Alexander Ross, architect, Inverness. Courtesy of K. MacLeman.*

the rank of Lieutenant, returning to Rosehaugh in 1884 to join his father and James Douglas.

It is inconceivable to think that James would have left his considerable wealth in young and inexperienced hands, and both young men spent a period on the estate, under the guidance of their father.

Alexander Ross, the Inverness architect much favoured by James, was commissioned to alter Rosehaugh House, and he added a porch facing south, and a conservatory to the east as final touches to a complete casing of the existing building (see illustration 15). Alexander Ross, known as the 'Christopher Wren of the North', was a long-lived and highly prolific architect. He has been credited with 650 commissions, yet very few records of his practice survive and none of his plans for Rosehaugh.

Woolton Hill House and Rosehaugh Estate did not satisfy James's appetite for acquiring and improving residential properties and in February 1877 Letham Grange in Forfarshire was added to his considerable property empire. Purchased from the Trustees of John Miln Hay for the sum of £121,800 it was already a house of great dimensions but, as on other occasions, James proceeded with plans for enlargement and reconstruction, incorporating the existing house with the addition of two wings. He engaged the Inverness architect John Rhind and employed Harrow and Sinclair as masons and Tulloch as painters, also from Inverness. Fern Estate also in Forfarshire was added to that of Letham Grange at this time.

While building his property empire in Scotland, James continued to manage his merchant trading business in Liverpool until 1884, though a Peruvian War with Chile in 1869 and lessening demand for alpaca wool due to changes in fashion caused him to diversify his investments. The interests of Fletcher & Co. in Arequipa were transferred to the ownership of Don Jose V Rivera, formerly their clerk there and in 1884, prior to drafting his will, James wrote to Don Jose relieving him of the £5000 debt still owed. James's business transactions continued to be conducted world-wide with large investments in mines and railways particularly in the London & North West Railway Company.

Having enjoyed reasonable health throughout his life apart from failing eyesight which an operation in London in 1884 only fractionally improved, James's death on 1 October 1885 was unexpected, especially as he had been due to turn on Avoch's new street lighting on 30 September and a visit to Letham Grange had been planned for the day he died.

On a wet and dismal day on 9 October, James Fletcher set out from his beloved Rosehaugh on his final journey along the top drive, eastwards from the House to the village and the family vault, which he himself had commissioned at the Parish Church (see illustration 16). Brief services had already been conducted at Rosehaugh, in the Drawing Room by Rev. MacDowall, Rosemarkie, and outside by the Rev. MacKerchar, Avoch. The coffin, consisting of layers of silk, lead, pine and beautifully polished oak, lay in state in the Hall almost hidden by the number of wreathes. Punctually at one o'clock the cortege moved from the house with the chief mourners, James Douglas, Fitzroy Charles and Edward Stephen, his sons, accompanied by nephews William Henry and Charles Fletcher, Brodie of Edinburgh, solicitor, Mr G Leslie and Mr T.F. Hamilton: these eight were the pall bearers. Local businesses had closed and people came from all over the Black Isle, swelling the assembled crowd to close on a thousand, all wishing to pay their last respects to a man who had been a benefactor to many of them. Representatives from as far as Elgin, church leaders and Highland gentry all attended. As the coffin was removed from the hearse at the bottom of Knockmuir Brae, Rev. Spence Ross, Fortrose, Rev. Chambers, Halewood, Liverpool and Rev. Eden, Inverness preceded it for the remaining part of the

16. *The Fletcher family burial enclosure, Avoch Parish Church.*

journey. Both Rev. Spence Ross and Rev. Chambers were visibly affected as they conducted the burial service and laid their long-standing friend to rest beside his son, Alfred Nevett, who had died only the previous year.

Shrewd, ambitious, generous, amiable, of vigorous intellect, loyal to his roots, supportive to many - James Fletcher was described as all of these. He laid the foundations for his sons to build on, but he also presented them with an incredible challenge - how to emulate such an example.

James's total estate amounted to more than £1,394,000 and his will made in May 1884, was extensively written for the guidance of his Executors and protection against all eventualities. When alive he had been liberal in his financial support of education, charities and individuals and his will, when executed, would continue to do so after his death.

Charitable legacies mentioned included the sum of £500 for the Northern Infirmary of Inverness and £2000 for charitable purposes in Liverpool with a further £2000 bequeathed to create the Rosehaugh Bursary for the benefit of a boy or boys attending Killen Primary and Avoch Junior Secondary schools 'such as showed promise and should continue to university'. To the individual its value was £30 per annum and it is still in existence though now available to any pupil in Ross-shire. In the month following his laying of the foundation stone at Elgin Academy, James added a codicil to his will allowing £2000 for a Fletcher Bursary which was to help the most distinguished pupil at Elgin Academy to continue to university.

One of the witnesses to this codicil signed at Rosehaugh was Roderick MacDonald, a trusted servant who had been with James for 13 years, first at Rosehaugh, then at Woolton Hill House, Liverpool, where, in seven years, he rose from footman to the position of butler and then valet to Alfred Nevett. Roderick had married in Liverpool but his young wife and infant son died within

18 months of his return to Rosehaugh in 1882. Remaining in James's service until James died, Roderick was rewarded with a bequest of £100 and the tenancy of Newton Farm.

Staff only recently in James's employment were to receive £20, but long serving house staff along with his warehouse keeper at Liverpool were given £50 per annum for life. Further bequests of between £500 and £3000 were made to godsons, nieces, widows and friends, his personal secretary at Liverpool and the Rev. MacKerchar of the Free Church, Avoch.

Arrangements for his children were of necessity detailed at great length, codicils being added in October and November 1884 after the death of the eldest son, Alfred. In the original will, drawn up before Alfred's death, James had made a final effort to correct his son's errant ways by bequeathing him an oil painting of Alfred himself as a little boy of five and by restricting his annual allowance at the age of 31 to £1000, the capital to remain in trust for 20 years.

Accepting that his son, Edward Stephen, would never inherit, James left £50,000 in trust for his 'maintenance and personal support' and Edward lived comfortably at Birkhill, Earlston, in the Borders, surviving to the age of 48.

Provision was made for Constance Maud in a £60,000 trust which annually released £600 for her 'maintenance and personal support' with the residue passing on her death to Caroline Violet, James's only grandchild, and her issue, for their maintenance, education or advancement. Little is known of the remainder of Constance Maud's life except that she died in 1914.

It was only in a later codicil that James Douglas and Fitzroy Charles were appointed executors along with the original ones who were Sir Archibald Leven Smith, Master of the Rolls, Judge of the High Court of Justice and husband of Isabel Fletcher, James's niece from Dale Park;

Charles John Fletcher, James's nephew from Dale Park; and finally Thomas Irving, a stockbroker from Liverpool.

Both James Douglas and Fitzroy Charles were to receive annual allowances of £5000 and £6000 respectively and the use of the family homes, but the residue was to remain in trust until they were 35. James Douglas inherited Woolton Hill House and the Rosehaugh Estates whereas Fitzroy inherited those of Letham Grange and Fern.

James died before the work was completed at Letham Grange and Fitzroy, under the terms of the will, had to finalise the improvements, furnish the house and plant the estate, all of which greatly added to the amenities. Fitzroy not only carried out his father's instructions but also continued with costly additions to the general estate which ran parallel to those taking place at Rosehaugh under James Douglas – erecting of hothouses; establishing a stud for race horses; installation of turbine generated electric light; building a fully equipped model dairy and, as a novelty, a miniature railway. His interests were similar to those of his brother and he too had success in agriculture and breeding prize cattle, but his favourite pursuit was hunting and for that purpose he rented Slane Castle in Ireland for several years, finally purchasing Ardmulchan Estate in County Meath where he embarked upon the building of a large residence for which the stone was quarried at Letham, dressed and shipped to Drogheda. Latterly, his long term heart condition limited travel and he had to rely on James Stirling, manager at Letham Grange, to co-ordinate with Sydney Mitchell, architect of the construction at Ardmulchan. Fitzroy's death at 44 years preceded the completion of his mansion in Ireland.

Fitzroy had inherited many aspects of his father's character in being shrewd, capable and generous with the added gift for public speaking which he used to advantage during local Council elections, being a Justice of the Peace and Deputy Lieutenant of the County of Forfar. Fitzroy did not, however, achieve success with his deep friendship with Ellaline Terriss, an accomplished and very beautiful London actress, who decided that Scotland was too remote and did not appeal to her. She returned to the attractions of the City and in 1893 married Seymour Hicks, who was to become Sir Seymour Hicks in 1934.

In 1890 Fitzroy married Frances Mary Grant, daughter of the Hon James MacPherson Grant of New South Wales. When Fitzroy died in 1902 of a protracted illness, her son, Conway Grant Fletcher, Fitzroy's stepson, inherited Letham Grange. The latter had already gained experience through extensive travel and time as a tea planter in Ceylon.

On Conway's death in 1957 the Trustees of the Fletcher Trust administered the estate. In 1973 they applied for planning permission to convert it to a leisure and country club with an 18 hole golf course.

Though James Douglas was to inherit Woolton Hill House as well as Rosehaugh, the 28 year old preferred to pursue his sporting and agricultural interests in the Highlands and let the house in Liverpool to various tenants before finally selling it. Rosehaugh was a magnificent property by any standards, and James Douglas a most eligible bachelor, but in 1890 the House still lacked a mistress. Fletcher's attentions were attracted by the vivacious Nellie Bass, heiress to the Bass brewing fortune and daughter of Baron Burton. However an alliance was never to take place, as, on being guided on a tour of the house, legend has it that she commented, 'My father provides better accommodation for his horses'.

Such a spurning of his intentions must have deeply wounded his pride. In 1892 James Douglas was 35, and under the terms of his father's will came into full control of his capital. By 1893 a selection of architectural plans had been drafted for the construction of a mansion house to supersede all others.

Meanwhile, on 31 January 1894, Nellie Bass married James Evan Bruce Baillie of Dochfour.

# Chapter 5: William Flockhart

SOON after he became laird of Rosehaugh, it must have become increasingly apparent to James Douglas that the house he had inherited, whilst it had served generations of MacKenzies, and with some alterations, been quite adequate for his father, was not really in keeping with his own tastes. He was a man who looked to wider horizons for inspiration and, by inclination and education, aspired to a world of culture and art unknown to his worthy, but eminently practical, father. He had more than one scheme of enlargement drawn up, including one unsigned, but bearing the hall-marks of the Inverness architect, John Rhind, who had drawn up the plans for the enlargement of the mansion house at Letham Grange in Forfar for James Fletcher. Perhaps Rhind's death in 1886 prevented anything further being done, but, in the event, J.D. Fletcher turned to London, where his friends and colleagues resided, and commissioned the Scots-born architect William Flockhart to draw up plans for Rosehaugh.

For almost 30 years, from 1881 to 1913, William Flockhart and the practice he founded, made a significant contribution to the architectural scene in London and

*17. William Flockhart – 1854-1913. Portrait by Elliot and Fry, court photographers. Courtesy of Mrs Christine Loeb, Flockhart's grand-daughter.*

18. *Chair designed by William Flockhart for Wylie &*
*Lochhead at the Glasgow Exhibition of 1888. Courtesy of Dr*
*Alastair Ward.*

many other parts of Great Britain. What is particularly interesting about his work is that he was not only an architect, but also an interior designer who designed and remodelled the interior furniture and decoration of rooms. His skills as a draughtsman and as a water-colour artist are mentioned by Stanley Adshead, one of his pupils, who himself became a distinguished architect. Flockhart was a man always striving to create perfection by using the best materials and expecting the highest standard of workmanship. His extensive knowledge of historical French and English styles, which he would combine together, meant that his designs were original though not of a pure architectural style. He was not a man to design anything plain, but using his knowledge, he would add extra windows, buttresses or bays, sometimes giving his creations a 'fairy tale' appearance. There is no doubt that these influences were clearly seen in Rosehaugh, which Flockhart was commissioned to remodel in 1893.

William Flockhart was born in Glasgow in 1854, the son of a chemist. He attended Glasgow Academy and studied architecture at the Glasgow School of Art. He was first apprenticed in Glasgow from 1870-1875 to Adamson and McLeod after which he moved to the offices of Campbell Douglas and Sellars, also in Glasgow, working as an assistant. By 1878 he had moved to London to design for a furniture manufacturer. During this period he gained knowledge of English and French styles by studying at the South Kensington Schools and by spending six months in Paris studying art, mainly in the museums.

In 1879 Flockhart joined William Wallace, another Scot, at Old Bond Street, London, first as an assistant then as a partner. In 1880, he married Christina Jane Lockhead, whose grandfather, John Lockhead, was a well known civil engineer of his day. In time, the Flockharts had one son and two daughters.

The following year, in 1881, he made the important decision to set up on his own account. It was not long before he made his mark on his chosen profession and in later years was described by Goodhart-Rendel, the architectural critic and commentator, as *'an extremely sensitive draughtsman, potentially the best of the lot'.* [10]

In addition, he passed on his skills, knowledge of styles, originality and his sense of perfection to his pupils. This can be seen particularly in the work of his pupils such as Charles Mallows (1864-1915), Stanley Adshead (1868-1947) and later in Oliver Hill (1887-1968), who was Flockhart's pupil from 1907 to 1910. Those who worked with Flockhart spoke of his highly strung artistic temperament and he seemed to have few real friends. His nature, according to his pupils, did not make him easy to work for. His desire for perfection frequently meant that he would erase his draughtsmen's work to produce a completely new idea. Understandably, this led to friction in the office, which, it is said, he would solve by 'buying off' the men with cheques.

By 1900, Flockhart's practice had become eminently fashionable as is evidenced by the clientele, almost all of whom were rich or titled or both. One of his earliest works in London was in 1886 for Elliot and Fry, the court photographers. He was commissioned to remodel their studios at Old Brompton Road, which he did in Early Renaissance style. Other work followed over succeeding years including 3 Hertford Street (the site of which now forms part of the garage of the London Hilton) for Sir Frederick J. Mirrielees, chairman of the Union Castle Shipping Line, and this house was subsequently acquired by James Douglas Fletcher. In 1893 Sir Frederick commissioned him to design Pasture Wood, Holmbury St Mary, Surrey, which was added to in 1906 by the famous architect Sir Edwin Lutyens, who later designed the Fletcher's burial ground in Rosehaugh in 1928.

In 1900, Flockhart entered the first of a number of architectural competitions with varying success. In 1901 he was made a Fellow of the Royal Institute of British Architects,

serving for several years as a Member of their Council and on their Finance Committee, acting as chairman for part of the time. Commissions continued in a steady flow including work for Sir Edmund Davis, a well known diamond merchant and art collector of the time. He also worked at Kinfauns Castle in Perthshire for Sir Donald Currie, another chairman of Union Castle Mail Steamship Company. Apart from Rosehaugh, this would appear to be the only job of substance Flockhart did in Scotland.

Flockhart's interests were diverse. As architectural adviser to the engineer for the Derwent Valley Water Board, he prepared designs for the Howden and Derwent dams. He was also appointed architect to the Union Castle Mail Steamship Company, in which capacity he was commissioned in 1910 to decorate and furnish the principal rooms aboard SS Balmoral Castle. This twin-screw steamer was the latest addition to the Union Castle fleet, in which it was planned that the Prince of Wales would make a voyage to South Africa in the autumn of 1910. The death of King Edward VII in May of that year, meant that the Prince of Wales became King George V, resulting in the Duke of Connaught taking the voyage instead.

On 10 April 1913, at the age of 59, Flockhart died at his home in London. His practice was continued by his son-in-law Leonard Rome Guthrie. Guthrie had also started his career in Glasgow and soon after the turn of the century had become a partner in the practice.

Among the final tributes to Flockhart and his work, was one given to the Royal Institute of British Architects at a General Meeting by E. Guy Dawber, acting for the Honorary Secretary. Part of what he said perhaps sums up Flockhart and his work:

*'Mr Flockhart was an able and brilliant architect; he was, moreover, a competent critic, tolerant and broad-minded and a passionate lover of the arts'.* [11]

19. *Rosehaugh House and Terraces. Original plan for remodelling, William Flockhart, 1893. Courtesy of K. MacLeman.*

# Chapter 6: The Exterior

THE story of the rejection of James Douglas by Nellie Bass may well be hearsay, but something certainly seems to have possessed him in his determination to make his house and estate the very 'pinnacle' of perfection. No expense was to be spared in designing and executing ever more elaborate designs.

A major internal refurbishment to Rosehaugh House had been finished in 1893 and Flockhart may well have been involved because his name is mentioned in a letter from John Henderson, the factor, dated 1888, in connection with obtaining some special tiles for the repair of a fireplace.

The house which now faced Flockhart was a four-square three bay house taking up the space shown on the plan later devoted to the Dining Room, Business Room, Morning Room, Library and Kitchen. It had a large projecting porch leading to the Hall, subsequently to become the Business Room. The exterior was in a style very far from Flockhart's, and it is not unreasonable to suppose that his inclination would have been to demolish the building and start from scratch. However it was decided to keep the original house and encase it. The original design is shown in illustration 19. This shows a relatively modest and cohesive house with a simple terrace. The architect planned to extend the house eastwards, with a completely new wing running northwards into the hillside. This would contain, in Flockhart's own words:

*'a new Hall, Drawing Room, Billiard and Smoking Rooms etc. on the ground floor, with swimming pond and complete arrangements for Turkish bath in the basement and the entire re-modelling and casing of the old house'.* [12]

The building contract was awarded to Foster & Dicksee of Rugby.

The new wing was started in a fairly unassuming Scots vernacular style, but Flockhart's penchant for continually changing things, by, for example, adding bays in odd places, led to his extension being less impressive as an entity than his casing of the original house. As to the style adopted by the architect for his new work, the nearest recognizable influence would be that of French Renaissance, but it refuses to be rigidly categorized. It has already been noted that Flockhart disliked anything plain. His other passion was for fine materials and workmanship. These predilections, combined with a strong romantic sensitivity, produced a style all his own, perhaps best epitomized by his love of towers and soaring roofs, with which Rosehaugh was to be amply provided. As Flockhart's practice was based in London his visits to the Black Isle were of necessity limited, so one of his brightest assistants was deputed to act as clerk of works. This was Stanley Davenport Adshead who later was to become an architect of greater fame and influence than his master. In his autobiography, he tells how, after hav-

20. *Work in progress – the main entrance.*

ing worked for Flockhart for a year, he was sent to Scotland to act as resident clerk of works, in order to solve some problems which had arisen at a big house being built in the Highlands for 'the Chairman of the Highland Railway, Mr Douglas Fletcher'. He went for a few weeks, these stretched to months and eventually he stayed for four years. During his time in Avoch, he met one of the village school teachers who became his wife.

He describes the house as a huge one built of stone, practically quarried off the site. Flockhart had selected red sandstone for the general walling and a contrasting greyish cream sandstone for the dressings and architectural features. The general effect, under a roof of pink clay plain tiles, was stunning, particularly when seen from the Avoch road. Adshead goes on to tell how, at any one time, there were 150 masons and about as many carpenters, bricklayers and labourers working on the job. He stayed at a farm called Ballone, near Ormond Castle. Flockhart would come up for a few days every month or so, and stay in the habitable part of the house. It was hardly an exaggeration to say that directly he had arrived and looked around, everything was stopped. He never pulled anything down, but always had fresh ideas as to how it was to proceed. He at once began to make drawings of the new proposal and meantime Adshead kept the workmen going with bits of the new idea. When Flockhart went, having left behind a heap of sketches, his assistant worked for a month to get everything going,

*'and no sooner would everything be working quite smoothly, than Flockhart would appear again, and repeat the process. He was ever seeking perfection, and discarding what he had done. This constant change of mind was most trying, but I never resented having to do things over again, for I felt that the last was always the best.'* [13]

Without Adshead's loyalty and patience, it seems

21. Coach and Four in front of Rosehaugh. Courtesy of the Brodie of Brodie.

doubtful whether the project would ever have been completed. He thought all this was excellent training, but considered that it put him back in many ways, especially as a competitor with men of his own age who were undergoing more conventional training in London. He eventually attained a high academic status, however, becoming Professor of Civic Design at Leverhulme in 1912 and, later, Professor of Town Planning at the University of London. Meanwhile after his departure from Rosehaugh, he was replaced as clerk of works by Leonard Rome Guthrie, Flockhart's son-in-law.

Let us take a brief tour round the outside of the House, starting with the east façade (see illustration 22). This is opulent and lacking cohesion and certainly provides a good example of the practices described by Adshead: it

22. *The House from the east (a later photograph with the balcony covered over).*

gives the impression of having been added to sporadically over a considerable number of years, whereas of course, it was built more or less continuously. The eastern end of the main frontage displays the same idiosyncrasies of style and the two-storied Jacobean bay which was eccentrically applied to the gable end is typical of Flockhart's somewhat perverse approach.

To the west of the controversial bay, the next feature, which was pure Flockhart, was a tower, 120 feet high. This was unadulterated fairytale fantasy encompassing pagoda roof turrets, overhanging balconies, miniature arcades, decorative friezes, extruded secondary towers: the list is endless. This confection was surmounted with a typical Flockhart soaring French château roof, which, in turn, was topped with a lead weather-vane in the shape of a two-masted brigantine, six feet high. It would be doing Flockhart less than justice, however, to dismiss the tower as mere extravagance. It performed the important role of housing the large, cold water tanks made necessary by the planned provision of vast amounts of piped hot and cold water. Moving westwards, the next 120 feet or so consisted of the casing of the original house and was relatively symmetrical, consisting, at ground floor level, of two flanking square bays, the eastern one being partially obscured by the main entrance porch. Between these the façade was recessed behind a triple arcade enclosing three balconies, two of which served the Dining Room and the remaining one the Business Room (see illustration 21). At first floor level the middle set of three windows was slightly recessed behind the line of the balconies. Finally, the second floor rooms were lit by three symmetrically placed and highly decorated lucarne windows. The remaining 10 feet or so of the façade, before the junction with the west front, were taken up with an arched window opening, whose twin formed the first feature of the return frontage.

The main entrance porch was approached by a flight of a dozen steps between two solid balustrades. The entrance steps led to a richly carved arched doorway whose semi-circular head was protected by a massive bracketed stone canopy also decorated with carving (see illustrations 23 and 30).

Carrying on round to the western façade, the roof at this end took a soaring form to complement that of the tower and the façade itself followed the general design of the main frontage, having two arches at ground level, behind which were the secondary entrance porch and vestibule (see illustration 24).

This would have been the regularly used entrance, leading to those rooms in daily use, whereas the entrance previously described led to the more ceremonial parts of the house. The first floor again followed the same arrangements as the main façade, having above two sets of mullioned windows, a pair of lucarne windows, the whole being balanced by yet another of Flockhart's characteristic roof forms.

No drawings survive giving details of the rear elevation (see illustration 26), but the floor plans show an entrance to the Kitchen Court, some structures of which remain to this day. The inhabitants of this House enjoyed a building on the exterior of which no expense had been spared – and on entering the house, they came into an interior fitted out, decorated and furnished with even greater opulence.

*23. South-west corner of the House.*

24. The House from the west showing main drive and the entrance to the Kitchen Court. Courtesy of the Brodie of Brodie.

25. The carving of a farmer on one of the walls of the house.

26. A rare view of the back of Rosehaugh. Courtesy of K. MacLeman.

*27. Rosehaugh from the west. Watercolour by Simon Mills.*

*28. A close view of some of the stone carvings round the house.*

*29. Intricate lead work on the gutters and down pipes.*

*30. The Front Door: Fitzroy Charles can be seen at the back left and a rear view of James Douglas is seen at the back right.*

# Chapter 7: The Interior

IT is now time to go inside – by way of the main entrance. At the top of the steps was an open porch which afforded a fine sitting-out place in good weather. To the left was a magnificent pair of panelled mahogany doors, with ornate carving and huge metal hinges, 10 feet high and 10 feet wide. Beyond lay a vestibule of similar proportions, which led by way of a short flight of steps to the Hall. There was also, off the vestibule, a door leading to the spiral staircase by which the tower could be reached. The Hall, which also served as the Ballroom, was a vast space, measuring some 50 feet by 25 feet. It had a magnificent oak suspended floor, probably one of the first of its kind and was appointed in what is often called the decadent English style: excessively heavy wooden ceiling and wainscot panelling, featuring an octagonal motif echoed in the panels of the massive cased double doors. So as not to interrupt the symmetry of this space, there was a large inglenook fireplace in a recess measuring nearly 20 feet by 8 feet in the north west corner. The fireplace itself was Elizabethan, 9 feet high and 9 feet wide, of stone and bore the date 1590. According to the *Building News* of December 1903, it came from the old Palace of James VI (I of England) at Bromley, Kent. There were two stained glass windows lighting the recess which also appear to be of some antiquity. Illustration 38 shows clearly the wooden ceiling and the floor is covered with a huge Indian carpet. Other features

*31. A group in the porch. Courtesy of the Brodie of Brodie.*

include an organ recess and a passenger lift to the upper floors - quite a rarity in a private house at that time. Beside this was a luggage lift with access from the servants' staircase to the upper floors. Off the Hall to the south was an ante-room with its own access into the Drawing Room.

Leading off the Hall to the east through a pair of ornate doors was the Drawing Room. This measured 42 feet by 24 feet, and had two bays, the larger of which measured 16 feet by 12 feet. Reference has already been made to the

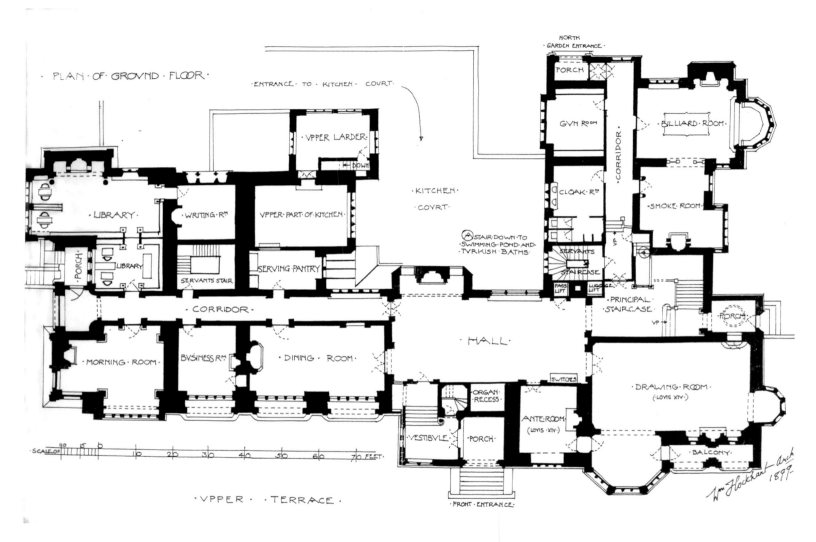

PLAN · OF · GROUND · FLOOR ·

ENTRANCE · TO · KITCHEN · COURT ·

NORTH
GARDEN ENTRANCE ·

PORCH

VPPER LARDER ·

DOWN

GVN ROOM

BILLIARD · ROOM

LIBRARY

WRITING · RM

VPPER · PART · OF · KITCHEN

KITCHEN

COVRT ·

CLOAK · RM

CORRIDOR

SMOKE · ROOM ·

LIBRARY

PORCH

SERVANTS STAIR

SERVING PANTRY

Ⓐ STAIR · DOWN · TO ·
SWIMMING · POND · AND ·
TVRKISH · BATHS ·

SERVANTS
STAIRCASE

VP

· CORRIDOR ·

PASS
LIFT

LVGGGR.
LIFT

MORNING · ROOM ·

BVSINESS RM

DINING · ROOM ·

HALL

PRINCIPAL
· STAIRCASE ·

VP

PORCH

SWITCHES

DRAWING · ROOM ·
(LOVIS XIV ·)

ORGAN ·
RECESS

ANTE · ROOM ·
(LOVIS · XIV ·)

VESTIBVLE

PORCH

SCALE OF

10  15  0        10        20        30        40        50        60        70 FEET

Wm Flockhart Arch
1899

BALCONY

· VPPER · TERRACE ·

FRONT · ENTRANCE ·

32. Ground floor plan, William Flockhart dated 1899.

42

effect of the added bays on the appearance of the house. One, the larger, was on the south wall of this room adjoining the fireplace. These two features took up the whole of this side of the room, making the reason for Flockhart's apparent eccentricity quite obvious. The other bay is on the east wall and it is difficult to fathom just why the architect chose to position it out of centre. Moving it a few feet to the north would have improved the symmetry not only of the room itself, but of the exterior of the eastern façade. However, the room, particularly when used in conjunction with the adjoining Hall on high days and holidays, must have been a sheer delight. The style was full-blown Louis XVI, the walls being panelled in French rococo boiserie, imported from Paris by the Duveens, the firm of antique dealers in London, whose showroom on Bond Street had been designed by Flockhart. The decorative friezes depicted, among other classical events, Venus with cherub attendants. The fireplace did justice to its setting, being of veined marble and ormolu. It can just be seen in our photograph to the left of the lady in the Louis XV fauteuil (see illustration 44).

Among other items supplied by the Duveens was a set of original Boucher tapestries for the Drawing Room with chairs to match. The elder Duveen came to Rosehaugh to supervise the installation and spent some hours pacing the room from end to end muttering 'my tapestries, my beautiful tapestries!' They also supplied many other items of 'choice and elegant French furniture' for the Drawing Room.

The door in the north eastern corner opened onto a small porch leading in turn to the main staircase. Whilst it had been planned to build a corridor to the east which would have led to the vast Palm House shown on some of the drawings, this was never built. We do not know why these plans were not carried out, but there was a large Palm House incorporated in the range of glasshouses built in the walled garden.

*33. Inside the main front door.*

43

*34. The Hall: showing the wooden ceiling, the doors into the drawing room and the bottom of the main staircase.*

*35. The Hall: the fireplace.*

*36. The Hall showing clearly the Indian carpet.*

*37. The Small Ante Room.*

*38. The Hall: c1900, showing the Indian carpet and a large tapestry to the left. Courtesy of the Brodie of Brodie*

*39 The Drawing Room: a group relaxing.*

40. *The Drawing Room showing the furnishings (top left).*

41. *The Drawing Room showing furnishings and the bay window (above).*

42. *The Drawing Room looking into the larger bay (left).*

43. *The Billiard Room: the walls in Moroccan leather. The doors into the Smoke Room.*

The decorative scheme of the Principal Staircase was in sympathy with that of the Hall. The wood-carving was remarkable, even by Rosehaugh standards and it was teamed with carved stonework of a similarly high order, together with a good deal of exquisite wrought-iron work, embellishing balustrades, balconies and other openings. The staircase itself had 29 treads of finest chestnut, each 7 feet three inches wide, and a moulded brass handrail, the polishing of which must have been a job in itself!

A pair of doors to the north gave access to the exclusively male domain of Smoke Room and Billiard Room. The first of these, the Smoke Room, was a relatively cosy 25 feet square, panelled from floor to ceiling in cedar decorated with ormolu strapwork. The floor was of Italian veined white marble.

A pair of doors, highly carved with chiselled ormolu, set in a partially glazed screen, led to the Billiard Room, which, in terms of decoration, was perhaps the most fantastic in this cornucopia of fantasy. A fairly plain panelled wainscot was surmounted by a wall covering of richly tooled Moroccan leather in a profuse fruit and flower design, predominantly in brown relieved with green and gold. Above this was a plaster frieze moulded in bas relief, depicting scenes from chivalry. The ceiling was in the form of an ornate plaster dome. To compete with all this the fireplace had to be something special. Measuring 13 feet six inches high by 11 feet nine inches wide it was surmounted by a stone plaque depicting The Seasons. It bore the motto 'HIC AEDIBUS PROSIT DEUS' – 'May God bless this hearth and home' and was dated 1897. For the benefit of spectators, there was a dais in the semi-octagonal bay window. In such lush surroundings, it must sometimes have been difficult to keep one's eye on the ball!

Across the passage from the Billiard Room lay the Gun Room. Together with the adjacent Cloak Room, this was

44. *The Drawing Room c1900. The young lady asleep in a Louis XV fauteuil (lot 674 in the 1954 sale – see page 69). The fireplace can just be seen on the right. Courtesy of the Brodie of Brodie.*

situated by the northern entrance, which would have been the one used by the shooters returning from a day's sport.

This entire section of the house provided a cosy male enclave and very much reflected the priorities of its bachelor owner. Continuing back along the passage there was a staircase leading down to the basement and the Swimming Pond, as it was called, and the Turkish Baths. These were planned so that despite being below ground they were naturally lit by high level conventional windows. The entrance was guarded by two bronze elephants 'as big as ponies' (see illustration 161). Most of the wall surfaces were lined with Italian marble, fixed by Italian craftsmen brought over for the purpose, and the cubicles were hung with exquisite mosaic tiles. There was a beautiful Italian marble drinking fountain 7 feet high and a marble fireplace.

45. *The bottom of the main stairs showing the corridor towards the Smoke Room.*

46. *The Smoke Room – panelled in cedar, with ormolu strapwork.*

47. *The Turkish Baths.*

48. *The Swimming Bath. All three photos courtesy of the Brodie of Brodie.*

In 1894 James Douglas Fletcher had become a member of the Baths Club in Dover Street, London, which was instituted:

*'for the purpose of affording to its members and their friends the usual privileges of a first class club, and providing for their use in connection therewith Turkish, Russian, Swimming and other Baths, together with facilities for Fencing, Gymnastics and recreative exercise at all seasons, under cover'.* [14]

The Club, now defunct, changed its name not long after to the Bath Club. At this time these facilities were most unusual in any private house in Scotland, although there was a swimming pool at Skibo Castle, built further

51

*49. Roof window in the Swimming Pool and Baths area.*

*50. The Dining Room, the pair of doors into the Hall.*

51. *The Dining Room, west end showing fireplace and door leading to the corridor.*

52. *The Dining Room c1900. Courtesy of the Brodie of Brodie.*

53. *The Business Room: showing the built-in safe.*

north near Dornoch by J.D. Fletcher's friend Andrew Carnegie.

The remainder of the rooms on the ground floor are all within the curtilage of the original house. If we recross the hall and go west down the main corridor, the first of these is the Dining Room. This was the only room at Rosehaugh to achieve the Palladian ideal of the double cube, its dimensions being 34 feet by 17 feet by 17 feet. It was sumptuous to the point of heaviness and James Douglas Fletcher's niece, Lilian Elford, later to become Mrs Shaw of Tordarroch, was to say that dining there was like eating in an Italian Renaissance chapel. Our photograph shows this clearly (see illustrations 50 and 52).

The walls were panelled to a height of about 8 feet in an ornate pattern which was painted green, enriched with gold leaf. The panelling was topped by a heavily moulded rail above which the wall surfaces were hung with Italian cut velvet in bottle green on a buff background. The fireplace was of white Italian marble, with the upper panels carved to represent scenes of warriors in battle. The ceiling was coffered into panels, oval and octagonal, all being richly decorated with scenes from classical mythology. Although, as has been noted earlier, this room had two balconies, there was no access to them, short of clambering over the window sills.

Next to the Dining Room on Flockhart's plan was the Business Room. This was panelled from floor to ceiling in oak; remarkably elegant with gilt rococo decoration, but one cannot help thinking that Flockhart would have done something quite different, had he guessed that within a very few years this room which had been the Hall of the original house would have become the Tea Salon. Only a large built-in safe betrayed its former purpose.

'Charming' is not a word that seems appropriate in describing this monumental house, but if there is to be an exception it is in relation to the Morning Room. Measuring 30 feet by 22 feet, it lay at the south west cor- ner of the main front. It was exceptionally well lit, having windows facing south and west. Its flavour was of the 18th century. There was a restrained dado painted in a pastel colour above which the walls were panelled out and hung with wall-cloth in a Regency stripe design. The centre of the ceiling was taken up with a large oval of plaster, the ribs of which bore a floral motif. This was supported on four sides by circular motifs of similar design and the whole was contained within cornices in keeping. Plaster ornamentation was also extensively used elsewhere in the room. Our photographs (see illustrations 54 and 56) show the ornamental plaster-work round the door and the French kingwood writing desk that appears as lot 525 in the 1954 sale. In the central oval of the ceiling was a fresco painted in situ by an Italian artist in the style of Angelica Kauffman, portraying Cupids in glory (see illustration 57). The fireplace was supported by a pair of caryatids, one male and one female and bore a central cartouche depicting Aesop's fable *The Wolf and the Sheep.*

Across the corridor and past the west side entrance was the Library. This occupied three rooms – including the Writing Room - and this is a legacy of the floor plan of the old house. This layout had a particular advantage in that it maximised the area of wall space available for book storage. The Writing Room was the one used by J.D. Fletcher as a study, once the Business Room had been redesignated as a Tea Salon.

It is calculated that over 10,000 volumes could have been accommodated, although the number listed in the 1954 auction particulars was a mere 3000. Every square inch of wall-space, bookcases, panelling and doors was in walnut and mahogany. The rooms had richly ornamented cornices supported by columns, some Corinthian and some Ionic: these too had a walnut finish. All the bookshelves were enclosed by glass doors, and were further protected by brass wire grilles. The fireplace was an imposing one with a stone canopy, bearing the monogram

*54. The Morning Room: c1900 showing the French kingwood writing desk (shown as lot 525 in 1954 sale). Courtesy of the Brodie of Brodie. See Page 141.*

*55. The Morning Room, south-west corner of the House, showing the fireplace and the fine plaster-work.*

'JDLF AD 1911'. It was flanked by two recesses fitted with banquette seats in buttoned leather. This fireplace, with its date and the initials of James Douglas and his wife Lilian, whom he married in 1909, must have been installed several years after the completion of the rest of the decoration.

Returning along the corridor to the east, a door on the left led to the Servants' Stair – the main stair of the original house. Next along the corridor was the entrance to the Serving Pantry, leading in turn to the Kitchen regions. The main kitchen measured 30 feet by 20 feet and extended through two floors, basement and ground, being lit by clerestory windows overlooking the kitchen court. It was adjoined by two larders, one at each level, and was connected to the Servery at ground floor level by a dumb waiter.

At the top of the principal staircase, there was a small

*56. The Morning Room, the door onto the corridor.*

landing on which a discreet door in the opposite wall concealed the way to the servants' stair and a room, marked 'Brushing' on the floor-plan, for storing larger cleaning utensils. The route to the right led through an ornate stone

*57. The Morning
Room Ceiling, style of
Angelica Kaufman.*

58

*58. The Main Library, showing the imposing fireplace, probably installed later.*

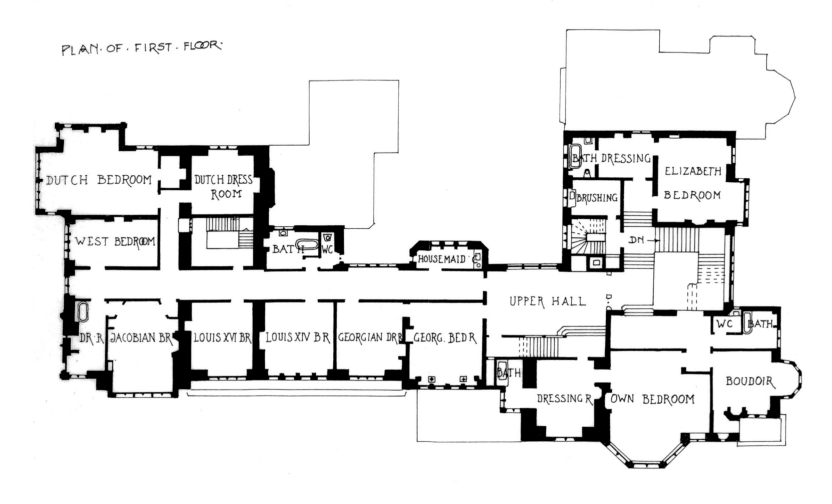

PLAN·OF·FIRST·FLOOR·

DUTCH BEDROOM

DUTCH DRESS ROOM

WEST BEDROOM

BATH

WC

HOUSEMAID

BATH DRESSING

BRUSHING

ELIZABETH BEDROOM

DN →

UPPER HALL

DR·R JACOBIAN BR

LOUIS XVI BR

LOUIS XIV B R

GEORGIAN DR R

GEORG. BED R

WC

BATH

BATH

DRESSING R

OWN BEDROOM

BOUDOIR

*59. The first floor plan, William Flockhart c1899.*

*60. The top of the main staircase, showing the 21-light window.*

and marble archway and up four steps to the Jacobean suite on the North side (marked 'Elizabeth bedroom' on plan). The room was clad in elegant oak panelling surmounted by a frieze of carved winged cherubs amidst foliage, upon which a valuable Spode dinner service was displayed round the room and in the corridor. Impressive though the mantelpiece was at 96 inches high by 84 inches wide and carved in the Elizabethan manner, the room's focal point was an imposing canopy from which hung heavily embroidered blue and white curtains, and below which the Elizabethan-style oak bed had a bedspread to match. To offset the darkness of the décor, the ceiling was in ornamental plasterwork (see illustration 64).

On returning to the head of the main staircase and turning left, four steps and a landing led both to the principal suite in the south east section and to the upper hall. Access to the south-east section was through another ornate stone and marble archway to a corridor where a glazed balcony permitted the viewing of those ascending the main staircase. This suite, marked 'Own Bedroom' etc. on plan, consisted of a bedroom, boudoir, dressing room and two bathrooms, amounting to some 3500 square feet.

The boudoir must have been a favourite spot with the early morning sun streaming in and lasting on the open balcony till afternoon. Carpeted in blue Wilton, a selection of easy chairs upholstered in lavender and grey tapestry, blue velvet and floral cretonne was complimented by floral chintz curtains and a second set of cream casement ones. A reminder of the commercial world was the presence of a large Milner's safe. With practicality in mind, the balcony was later built over.

The master bedroom measured 25 feet by 19 feet and contained a valuable inlaid mahogany suite, the wardrobe of which measured 10 feet two inches, in length. The curtains in floral design and cream matched those of the boudoir and worthy of mention was a floral and scrolled gilt wall mirror rising 8 feet nine inches high.

It would be remiss to omit mention of the bathrooms, or more specifically the baths, some of which were raised by two or three steps, one or two of which were recessed, most of which were surrounded by mirrors and marble, but all of which were of such a size that, when filled, would have covered the ample proportions of the largest Victorian lady. In later years Mrs Fletcher appreciated the wastefulness of the baths and had some lined with modern ones. The plan would seem to indicate that the bathroom adjoining the Boudoir boasted a fireplace, as indeed did the Jacobian bedroom.

The first storey was fitted throughout with oak strip flooring over which quality Wilton carpeting was laid, the exception being the principal staircase which was covered with extra heavy quality crimson Axminster. Many years later, and after many hundreds of feet had passed over them, these carpets were still in excellent condition.

Apart from the Dutch suite, the bedrooms or suites were decorated and furnished in different period styles, providing guests with the facilities of a private sitting room, and for those who had a suite, a dressing room with matching bedroom furniture and an extra bed. The outstanding fireplaces were mainly 18th century marble surrounded by pine, mahogany or oak mantelpieces.

From the principal suite, access to the other bedrooms was through the upper hall whence the 'comings and goings' of the back courtyard could be seen. The corridor, leading westwards from the upper hall was 109 feet long with bedrooms along the south side, and a maid's pantry on the opposite wall was hidden again behind a panelled door. Further along this same wall a bathroom was provided for the guests whose bedrooms did not have private facilities. This too may have had a fireplace.

Directly from the upper hall was the prime Georgian suite containing fine mahogany and satinwood banded furniture, a carved mahogany bed with two upholstered top panels in French brocade and velvet, a green Wilton

*61. The window in the Master Bedroom.*

bordered carpet and Persian rug, all of which can be seen in illustration 62. The main theme colour was pink and this was carried into the dressing room where the walls were lined with pale rose silk damask panels in Regency stripe.

Next door, the Louis XIV room was decorated with attractive oak indented panels inset with figured green silk damask, the colour being reflected in the verde antico marble fireplace. The bed canopy drapes of fine floral green silk damask matched the window curtains and complimented the three fold gilt screen of green and gold brocade.

Adjacent to the Louis XIV room, lay the Louis XVI bedroom with the William and Mary Tapestry suite occupying the south west corner (marked Jacobian on plan). The use of pine dominated the Tapestry suite with both rooms having doors, door-frames and wall panelling heavily and intricately carved. As in the Jacobean suite the mantelpiece was indeed impressive, rising to a height of 10 feet with the overmantel containing an oval cartouche of berried foliage, a design which was copied in the ornamental plaster ceiling. This room had a valuable antique canopied Elizabethan pillar bed.

The Dutch suite and a single west bedroom, both in the north west corner, completed the extensive choice of accommodation on the first floor. Here a staircase led to the top floor where there were further guest bedrooms along with a few servants' rooms. Even in this area the high standard of workmanship and quality was not neglected and the elegant oak wall panelling followed the staircase and round the top landing.

Of the 10 rooms at this level, five had a southern exposure, along with the most spectacular of views, amply compensating for their lack of facilities. The flooring at this level was of pine and the woodwork painted white, but comfort was catered for with crimson Wilton carpeting and the continuing high standard of furnishings in the five front rooms. The remainder of the top floor provided five rooms for servants, a house-maid's pantry and a large 20 feet by 12 feet store with cupboards.

The endless corridors, the numerous doors, stairs and corners would have made the first and top floors the most exciting of places for a child to play 'hide and seek' on a wet, dismal day.

One further important room remains to be described, and that is the Tower Smoke Room. This was reached by way of the staircase situated off the vestibule and was at the summit of the Tower behind the arcade. It was also known as the 'Summer' Smoke Room, and at that time of year, when the June twilight is endless, it must have been a most attractive place to which to retreat, and enjoy the spectacular views. It was panelled in oak, in a style which by comparison with some of the other rooms can only be described as fairly plain and masculine. The fireplace was of stone and the canopy was supported by a pair of caryatids, both female, whose postures were so contorted that the agony of doing their work could be read in their faces.

Those who remember the house invariably recall the wonderful fragrance of wood, particularly cedar wood. Even the corridors had wood panelling and polished oak floors. Another decorative feature is of particular interest. A few antique stained glass panels appeared at the sale, and we know from photographs that many of the windows had decorative leaded clear glass panels. However a mystery surrounds some other pieces of stained glass. William Flockhart had collaborated in 1888 with the Glasgow firm of stained glass manufacturers, J. & W. Guthrie, in the decoration and furnishing of a Scots baronial dining room for the firm of Wylie & Lochhead, at the Glasgow exhibition of that year. The firm designed a great deal of stained glass for Rosehaugh, the most outstanding of which was a 21-light installation which would have been for the Main Stair window (see illustration 60). A coloured sketch remains in the archives of the People's Palace in Glasgow showing a magnificent window, designed by David Gauld in a free adaptation of Hornel and Henry's painting *The Druids Bringing in the Mistletoe*. Gauld was later to achieve considerable fame as an artist. We simply do not know whether the designs were executed and installed, and then later removed; or whether they remained on the drawing board. Certainly no stained glass of this period ever appeared for sale. The photograph of the staircase window shows only the figure of a female warrior occupying three vertical lights, appearing incongruously in surroundings of plain glass.

The furnishings for all this decorative opulence were invariably in keeping with the style of each room. Flockhart's sketches show certain rooms and we have photographs of some others. The architect draws freehand the furniture in the rooms, and clearly his brief was

*62. The Georgian bedroom c1900. Courtesy of the Brodie of Brodie.*

63. *The archway and steps leading to the Jacobean suite ('Elizabeth Room' on plan).*

64. *The 'Elizabeth Room': the oak canopy.*

65. The Tower Smoke Room: the imposing stone fireplace.

66. The fireplace from the dressing room of the Georgian bedroom.

67. The Tower Smoke Room: the door to the stairs.

*68. The door to the William and Mary bedroom (marked Jacobian on plan).*

not just to remodel the house and design the decorative finishes, but also to decide on the furnishings. At this time James Douglas was still a bachelor. His factor, John Henderson, recalls in a series of reminiscences of his life at Rosehaugh that James Douglas relied on Lady St Helier, one of the leading society hostesses of her day, for advice on furnishing the house. Lady St Helier was born a MacKenzie from Brahan Castle, and married Francis Jeune, later Baron St Helier, a High Court judge. Although we know that they were visitors to Rosehaugh, it is not possible to distinguish any influence on the interior decoration of the house other than that of Flockhart.

The *Building News* of 1 January 1904, carried a report of the progress at Rosehaugh, and referred to the interior which it noted as being:

*'so full of works of art that it has been described as being almost a museum of antiquities'.* [15]

The summary of contents from the 1954 auction sale particulars gives some idea of the wealth of items. In addition, outside the house, on each side of the main steps were placed a pair of Burmese bronze chindits. These were probably installed around September 1902 (see illustration 74). In the same month, a number of other oriental bronze statues and other pieces were laid out along the top of the terrace (see illustration 73). The great Buddha also arrived at this time (see illustrations 1 and 72).

At the same time as the remodelling and redecoration of the House, new services were installed. The Killen Burn was dammed to provide, as well as a large lake, an electricity generating facility, supplying power to the House and some of the surrounding estate. Water from the burn was pumped, by electricity, into the huge tanks in the Tower. Central heating was provided by a warm air system, whereby the heated air was driven by a hydraulic engine and delivered by ducts and decorative brass grilles

# CATALOGUE
of
### The Highly Important and Extensive Sale by Auction
of
## The Contents
of
## The Mansion House of Rosehaugh, Avoch,
### Ross-shire
Which will be Sold on the Premises as instructed by the Proprietors.

*Comprising:*

VALUABLE ANTIQUE ENGLISH, CONTINENTAL, EASTERN and OTHER FURNITURE and FURNISHINGS.

THE CHOICE AND ELEGANT FRENCH FURNITURE OF LOUIS XV, XVI AND LATER PERIODS INCLUDES: Cabinets, Cylinder Top Escritoire, Writing Cabinet and Table, Suites of Gilt and Walnut Fauteuils in Beauvais Tapestry and Damask, Salon Clock by Robert, Clock Sets by Kinable and by Boudet, Wall Clock by Gudin, Boulle Desks and Tables, etc.; **Dutch and English Cabinets;** Library Bookcases, Desks, Secretaire and Tables; Georgian Mirrors; Elizabethan, Jacobean and Chippendale Design Dining Furnishings; Fine Screens, including One with Fine Panels of the Seasons by Burne Jones, and One of Chinese Incised Lacquer; Hall Furnishings and Clocks; the Furnishings of Boudoir and 24 Family Bedrooms and Dressing Rooms; **AN UNUSUALLY FINE LIBRARY OF BOOKS** on Sport, Botany, Art, History, etc., mostly in Choice Bindings by ZAEHNSDORF, RIVIERE and OTHERS, comprising Lawrance's Book on The Rose, Annals of Sporting, Lilford's Birds, Racinet's Costume, etc.; **COLLECTION OF INTERESTING SHIPPING PRINTS** in Line, Aquatint and Lithography by Canot, Dukes, Dutton and Others, Etc.; **VALUABLE OLD ENGLISH, CONTINENTAL AND ORIENTAL PORCELAIN AND POTTERY;** Dinner, Breakfast, Dessert, Tea and Coffee China; Cut Crystal and Table Glass; **BRONZE, BRASS AND COPPER;** Unique Collection of Rare German Stained Glass Panels of late XVI and early XVII Centuries; **Costly English, Persian and Indian Carpets;** Silk and Other Persian Rugs and Strips; Old Fire Backs; Billiard Table; Pianos; Gun Cabinets; Safe; Garden Furniture and Ornaments; Stone Fountain Head and Sundial; Horse Carriages and Traps; Carriage Lamps and Harness; **VALUABLE HOUSEHOLD NAPERY, BED AND TABLE LINEN,** CURTAINS; THE FURNISHINGS OF STAFF AND DOMESTIC OFFICES, Etc.,

which will be sold by

## THOMAS LOVE & SONS
On

**MONDAY,**    **TUESDAY,**    **WEDNESDAY,**    **THURSDAY and FRIDAY,**
23rd,      24th,      25th,      26th,      27th August

And on

**TUESDAY,**    **WEDNESDAY and THURSDAY** (if necessary)
31st August,      1st      2nd September, 1954.

Commencing ELEVEN o'clock Forenoon each day.

———

**ON VIEW—THURSDAY, FRIDAY and SATURDAY,**
19th      20th      21st August

10 a.m. — 4 p.m. each day.

Admission to View and Sale is by Catalogue only   -  -   Price 5/- each.

———

### TERMS CASH.

———

THOMAS LOVE & SONS, *Auctioneers and Valuators,* PERTH.
'Phones: Perth 2226 (3 lines)   or   ROSEHAUGH HOUSE, AVOCH: Munlochy No. 205.

*69. Page 3 of the Catalogue for the 1954 Rosehaugh sale.*

*70. Louis XV Carved Walnut Fauteuil. Lot 674.*

*71. Chinese Porcelain Bowl. Lot 641.*

to every room. Whilst it was extremely sophisticated for the period, the system suffered from inherent defects: it was noisy, the air was of doubtful purity, and it consumed a ton of coal a day. Virtually every room in the house had a fireplace as a second line of defence.

The remodelling of Rosehaugh House took 10 years and some £250,000. This far exceeded any other comparable scheme undertaken in Scotland at that time and partially reflects the cost of the lavish interior fittings and the works of art culled from all over the world. The work done at Skibo Castle for Andrew Carnegie (by the Inverness architect Alexander Ross who had worked for J. D. Fletcher's father) at about the turn of the century, cost only £100,000. Comparisons between the costs of various schemes of enlargement are almost meaningless, even when accurate records are available.

Rosehaugh was in more than one way an anachronism. The country house boom had come to an end with the agricultural slump of 1879-94 and an analysis of 500 country houses built or remodelled between 1835 and 1889 shows 36 in 1835, rising steadily to a peak of 74 in 1870-74. It then falls steeply to a low point of 26 in 1885-89, the very time that Rosehaugh was being developed. The few houses that were built in the early years of the twentieth century tended to be unostentatious.

At Rosehaugh an owner with almost unlimited funds and a burning desire to impress, met an architect with a passionate interest, not only in extravagant building, but in the finest of decorative materials and the most sumptuous of furnishings. The result was not pure or classical, but it was certainly extraordinary. No doubt both were well satisfied with the decade's work.

During the years since he had inherited from his father, James Douglas Fletcher had also, with the same dedication, turned his attention to transforming the gardens into suitable surroundings for his lavish Mansion House.

72. *The late Donald MacLeman in the presence of the Rosehaugh Buddha.*

73. *Japanese curiosities on the Terrace at Rosehaugh,1902. Courtesy of the Brodie of Brodie.*

74. *One of the pair of Burmese Bronze chindits: September 1902. At the main entrance to Rosehaugh. Courtesy of the Brodie of Brodie.*

*75. The garden staff of Rosehaugh c1910.*

# Chapter 8: The Garden

EVEN today, many years after the departure of the last gardener, the 'policies', to use the good Scots term, or the 'designed landscape' as present-day garden historians will have it, present a picture of harmony and fertility. Approaching on one of the entrance drives leading from the Munlochy-Avoch road the structure of the gardens and immediate woodlands, stripped of the distractions of flower-beds and garden statuary, becomes apparent: the site of the house, now an area of grass turf and birch seedlings, backed by fine coniferous planting; the tree-lined drives; the sweep of the grass parks down towards the Avoch road; the ornamental lake; the vast walled kitchen garden and the fine stone terraces: it is not difficult to imagine how it must have looked when a staff of 20 worked six-day weeks, with two days' holiday a year, to keep it all going. The years immediately before and after the First World War were probably the glory days; but when one considers the detail of estate maps and plans of the last 150 years, it becomes evident that this landscape has been designed and actively managed for a great deal longer. The 'perfecting' of Nature has been made easier here by the general aspect of the site:

*'Situate your House in a healthy Soyl, near to a fresh-spring, defended from the impetuous westwinds, northern colds and eastern blasts…'* [16]

These were the conditions laid down by John Reid, author of the first book on gardening in Scotland, *The Scots Gard'ner published for the climate of Scotland*, which appeared in 1683. Reid came from a long line of gardeners, and was employed on several large gardens in the south of Scotland before coming to work for Sir George MacKenzie of Rosehaugh on his estate of Shank, on a bank of the South Esk Water in East Lothian in 1680.

He stayed there for three years, and during that time must have been writing his small masterpiece, for in 1683, without even waiting to see it off the presses, he left with his wife and young family to settle in America. He worked in New Jersey as a surveyor, and ultimately laid out an estate of his own. There is no direct evidence that Reid ever worked at Rosehaugh itself; after all MacKenzie made only occasional visits and had other estates in Forfar to maintain. However, it seems unlikely that Reid's advice at least would not have been sought. His book contains, in addition to much practical advice on cultivation, directions for storing and preserving fruit, a 'gard'ner's kalendar' of the work to be undertaken throughout the year, detailed instructions on the laying-out of estates, avenues and gardens and precise mathematical formulae for achieving in all things the ideals of symmetry to which 17th century gardeners aspired. No remains of such a layout survive around the site of George MacKenzie's house; but the choice of site would

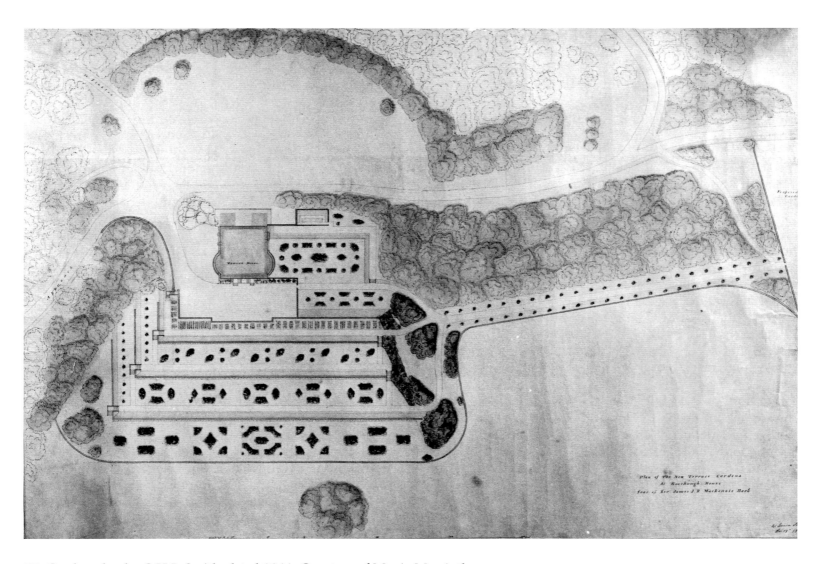

*77. Garden plan by C.H.J. Smith, dated 1844. Courtesy of Mr A. MacArthur.*

79. The Gardener's Cottage, built by Sir J.J.R. MacKenzie. c1850.

78. The gate towards the Slaughterhouse.

80. The garden wall and gate from the east.

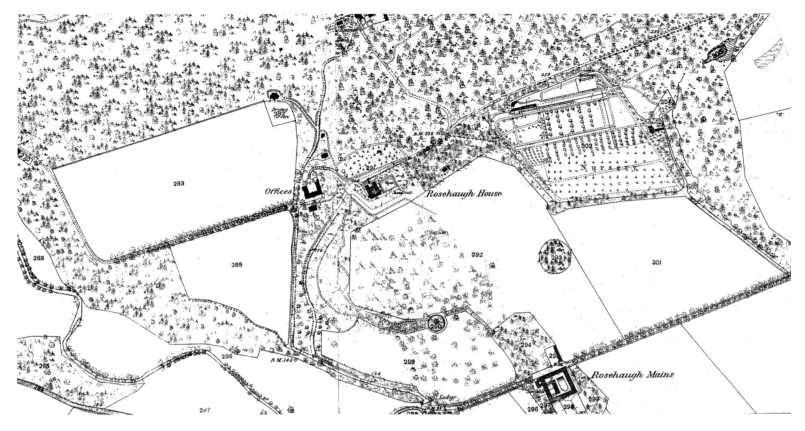

81. Section of the Ordnance Survey map, first edition, 1871, Rosehaugh House and the gardens.

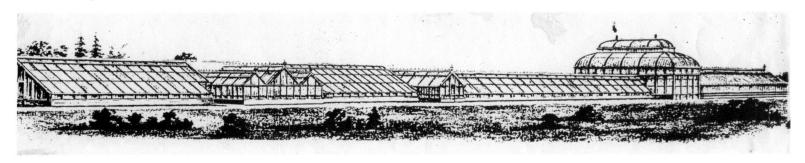

82. The Rosehaugh hothouses from the catalogue of MacKenzie and Moncur.

78

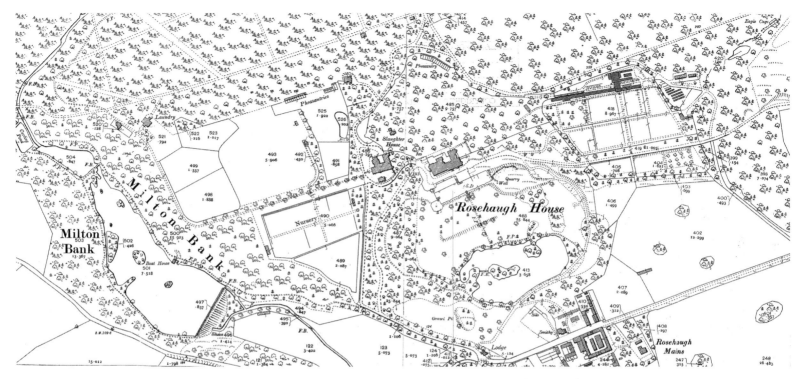

*83. Section of the Ordnance Survey map, second edition, 1904, Rosehaugh House and the gardens.*

revival of interest in more formal flower gardens close to the house at this time, a reaction against the free-flowing naturalistic landscapes of earlier years. However, this part of the design seems not to have been executed: a print from 25 years later shows only a gravel sweep. But, tantalizingly, just off the edge of this plan lies the walled garden, and a marker says 'new garden'. This magnificent six-acre garden was made, and, though desperately overgrown, still stands today. In November 1844 an advertisement appeared in the *Inverness Courier*:

'*Estimates Wanted: for ERECTING the GARDEN WALLS, HOTHOUSES, GREENHOUSES, PITS, GARDEN*

*OFFICES, EARTH WORK and FORMING DRAINS ETC in the New Garden at Rosehaugh, Seat of Sir J. J. R. MacKenzie, Bart'.* [19]

Sealed tenders were to be lodged with Mr Smith, 41 Queen Street, Edinburgh. By 1850 it had been built. A wall, which still exists, was made running from just north-west of the house, sweeping round to the east, enclosing the fine coniferous planting to the north of the house, and ultimately forming the north and west boundaries of the walled garden. It was a sturdy random rubble wall with moulded copings and arched gateways at appropriate places, and forms, together with the main

79

*84. Down the terrace steps.*

drives, a defined 'inner' policy landscape. The garden itself can be seen on the 1850 map, with paths and beds neatly laid out. At the top of the garden, in the north west corner, was a row of stone sheds and stores, built onto a secondary wall running west to east along the top of the garden and providing on its southern side support for a row of lean-to hothouses facing full south. Nor was the head gardener of this fine establishment forgotten: a good stone and slate cottage was built, still standing squat and solid today. Whilst the Sixth Baronet constantly lived well beyond his means, the work that he did on the estate was always practical, and most of the buildings, walls and bridges built in his time still stand intact after 150 years.

The next picture we have of the estate dates from the first Ordnance Survey Map of 1871 (see illustration 81). No vast landscaping work has been undertaken: the trees round the grass parks have grown and multiplied and a small circular area of conifers planted to form a feature on the eastern half of the park. A larger area north of the Mains Farm has been planted, perhaps to screen the farm and saw-mill from the house. There is even a small amount of garden ornament: a sundial in front of the house and a 'vase' on the small enclosed garden area adjoining the house to the east. There is also a sundial in the north eastern corner of the main walled garden which otherwise remains as it was 20 years before.

James Fletcher had a great deal of money at his disposal but he was a canny man and not one to indulge in garden extravaganza. He spent a great deal on practical improvements to the farms and wider estate and could afford to keep up the gardens to a high standard, with the employment of the large workforce this would have required. A. J. Beaton in the *Guide to Fortrose and the Vicinity* of 1885 records that Mr Fletcher permits visitors:

*'At all times to ramble freely through any portion of his splendid pleasure grounds and magnificent gardens.'* [20]

*85. A corner of the lower terraces.*

When James Douglas Fletcher inherited Rosehaugh in 1885, he had a well-set up estate waiting for him. With the vigour of youth, and urbane tastes, he set about the gardens with gusto. Almost immediately a fine range of hothouses was commissioned from MacKenzie and Moncur, premier glass-house manufacturers in Scotland at this time. The Rosehaugh greenhouses must have been outstanding, as they were used to illustrate their catalogue

*86. The bottom of the terraces and the path to the lake. Courtesy of James Gow, Fortrose.*

(see illustration 82). They extended almost the full length of the north side of the walled garden. The wood was teak, the fittings bronze and the floor mosaic tiles. One man remembers how, on a fine sunny day, from the other side of the Moray Firth on the Inverness to Nairn road you saw not the hothouses themselves, but the glare from the glass. In 1893 the members of the Inverness Scientific Society and Field Club visited Rosehaugh and recorded their impressions in their Transactions:

*'In the gardens, the extensive glass houses, where grapes, pineapple, melon and other fruit were growing luxuriantly, and where palms and exotic flowers contribute their shade and colour, excited special interest. The beautiful fernery also, arranged in shady grottoes, lined with moss and watered with cool streams, afforded a pleasant change from the hot sun outside.'* [21]

And all this north of the Highland Line!

The fernery, that most typically Victorian of garden features, was certainly outstanding. There are still many traces today. It must have measured 25 metres by 25 metres, including the flanking greenhouses on either side. The glass has caved in, the water no longer runs, but the artificial rockwork still remains, covered by a single species of fern: no doubt, thug-like, it has taken over from the wide variety that must have been planted here originally. One can still venture down the mossy steps onto the sunken pathways.

The heating in the greenhouses themselves was very sophisticated. Elaborate ducting carried hot water and an intricate system of hot air heating even within the walls, to provide the heat necessary for early fruit crops (see illustration 93). A vast range of cold frames was built to the east of the main garden wall, and espalier fruit trees must have covered the inner west wall of the garden, protected from early sun after a late frost. The biggest alter-

*87. The garden pony, c1900. Courtesy of the Brodie of Brodie.*

*88. Garden retaining wall showing drainage spouts.*

89. *The footbridge onto the island in the artificial lake. Courtesy of the Brodie of Brodie.*

ation to the kitchen garden was a track built east to west separating the lower third of the garden from the rest, no doubt completing a formal circuit drive or walk from which to show visitors the full extent of the policies. This lower part of the garden became grass parks, and cypress trees now line the southern wall of the truncated garden, once planted as a hedge, but now growing shoulder to shoulder 60 feet high. There is a fine stand of bamboo along this drive, and in spring this whole area is awash with daffodils, though by high summer the entire garden is smothered in weeds. Nothing else remains of the original flower and shrub planting, except for some ornamental rushes by the lake, ubiquitous rhododendrons lining the drives and more hedging, this time box, again run amok at the top of the terraces.

These terraces are still a magnificent sight. Designed by William Flockhart, they formed an entity with the house, in common with the designs of other architects working in Scotland at the time, for example, Robert Lorimer. Such is the quality of the stonework that after many decades of neglect, they still stand almost intact. At the top were small formal flower beds, clipped conifers stood to attention on the terraces themselves, and steps led down through a magnificent pair of bronze gates (see illustration 84) with urn-topped piers to a path with formal flower beds and J. D. Fletchers's beloved roses on either side and on towards the lake (see illustration 86). This lake, six acres in all, was under construction when the members of the Field Club made their visit:

*'They were interested in seeing the beginnings of a fish pond which Mr Fletcher is constructing, intended to cover six acres, and to be stocked with Loch Leven trout.'* [22]

An artificial island was made, complete with footbridge (see illustration 89). A path led round the small lake and back to the house, providing another walk. On

*90. William Mortimer Moir, head gardener. Courtesy of Dr C. C. Moir.*

*91. The son and daughter of W.M. Moir, in front of Slaughterhouse Cottage. Courtesy of Dr C. C. Moir.*

*92. Willie Chisholm,
last head gardener,
viewing his plants.*

the shores of the lake was a small wooden summer house (see illustration 109).

In 1903, a bazaar was held at Rosehaugh, to raise funds for the renovation of the harbour. It lasted for three days, and one of the main attractions was the 'Grand Illumination of the Lake and Terraces of Rosehaugh each evening at 7.30pm.'. According to the programme:

*'a visit should also be paid to the Gardens, with their unique rock-hewn ferneries, and the children will be interested to see the eagles in their big quarry home beyond.'* [23]

Many other landscaping works were undertaken by James Douglas Fletcher, mainly to provide a wide range of sporting activities for his own and his guests' enjoyment, and we shall discuss these later. But in the years just before the First War, the pleasure gardens at Rosehaugh were certainly at their formal best, tended by a small army of gardeners and assistants. The head gardener for much of this time was William Mortimer Moir. He went to Rosehaugh around 1892 and stayed until around 1920. We have him photographed (see illustration 90) in one of the greenhouses, and another photograph (see illustration 91) shows his son and daughter sitting outside Slaughterhouse Cottage where they lived. We also have a charming photograph of the 'garden pony' – a tiny Shetland with a miniature cart, piled with seed-boxes (illustration 87). The gardens were well-known in the north, and provided a great attraction when the public had access to the grounds for fêtes or for the Black Isle Farmers' Society Shows, and it was a point of honour for the gardeners to win the coveted cups and prizes at these shows. At one, in 1909, they exhibited no fewer than 25 varieties of potato.

Each new owner at Rosehaugh has shaped the landscape and rebuilt or remodelled the house according to the whims of his character, the style of the times and the

93. Interior of one of the greenhouses showing the heating system.

depth of his pocket. The gardens here have sustained generations of country families; now a very few estate workers remain. Times have changed. It is to be hoped, however, that the outstanding garden features that remain could be conserved and managed with an eye to the past as well as to the future, and that any new development would be in sympathy with the benign and lovely rhythms of the landscape.

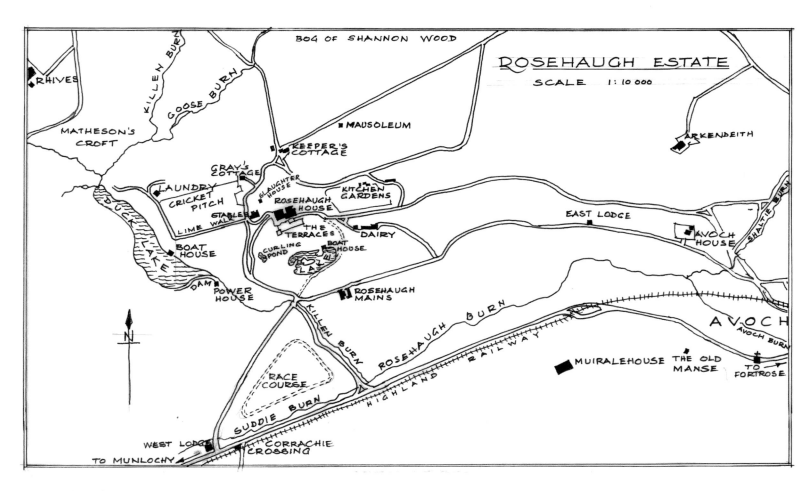

94. *Rosehaugh estate map.*

# Chapter 9: The Estate

THE well-managed country house estate of late Victorian times, built sometimes on inherited wealth, or on the proceeds of trade and industry, was a model of order and self-sufficiency. It was a little kingdom, in which the owner ruled as a benevolent despot, providing secure employment for many country families, and in return receiving lifetimes of devoted service. While there were strictly defined boundaries of propriety over which neither side would step, there was certainly a good deal of mutual respect. Generations succeeded one another, in the servants' cottages, as in the 'Big House'. The estate was run to be self-sufficient in all the basic requirements for living: housing, food, fuel; and for the servants, whilst hours were long and living conditions cramped, conditions were incomparably better than the squalor of the cities. For landowners, the estate also provided opportunities to indulge in all kinds of sporting activities, and, as we have seen at Rosehaugh, the chance to garden on a grand scale.

In all these respects, James Douglas Fletcher's estate was very typical. The huge kitchen gardens and hothouses provided a wide range of fruit and vegetables for the main house. To the east and just below the house a Dairy was built, said by some to have been based on the one at Sandringham. Designed by William Flockhart, its date of construction, at around 1907, makes it one of the last buildings to be put up on the estate. It consists of three parts: a house for the dairyman, a milking parlour and dairy and a byre, built of stone, partly ashlar, partly harled. These are linked by means of covered ways constructed of rough hewn oak under tiled peined roofs, of which the lower slopes are so flat that they are not completely weather-proof. The effect is immensely charming, enhanced with little touches such as the weather-vane with its art nouveau letters and the exquisite workmanship displayed in every detail. The dairy still stands today, as do most of the estate buildings, though many are now used for purposes other than their original ones. There was a small herd of a dozen Jersey cows and a bull; it was a registered stud, and ran independently of the Mains Farm. Two dairymaids not only made the butter and the cheese but also cleaned all the equipment needed to ensure almost limitless supplies of milk and cream to the House. During the War, the dairy supplied milk to the village. It was a requirement that some Ayrshire cows be kept to increase the yield and ensure the milk conformed to Ministry of Food specifications.

Near the stables was the slaughterhouse and cottage. This still stands, converted to living accommodation, and can be seen in illustration 114 with its distinctive untrimmed timber porch. Sheep, cattle and pigs were slaughtered here and hung, and then the carcases taken to a cold store in the kitchen regions of the main house. Bacon and hams were cured in brine in huge tanks situ-

95. *Middle section of The Dairy at Rosehaugh, used for making butter and cheese. Architect William Flockhart.*

*96. A complete view of The Dairy unit.*

ated in the heights of the Tower, where the circulation of cool air ensured good keeping. Enormous numbers of furred and feathered game were shot on the estate, and there is an octagonal timber game larder behind the kennels cottage. This cottage was the residence of the head game-keeper, but until recently was used as the estate office. It is a solid L-shaped cottage, built as part of J. J. R. MacKenzie's expansion in the 1840s and added to later. It has an unusual diagonally-set gable porch.

In addition to the cottages provided for the head gardener, head gamekeeper and dairyman, there were many other cottages on the estate, some of them now demolished. There is a range of bothies on the east side of the walled garden, probably for the unmarried male staff, and several families lived at the Mains Farm, in the once splendid quadrangle, built in 1812, housing the estate 'offices' and farmworkers' accommodation. There was a fine late Victorian farmhouse (1884) at the Mains for the

manager. The farmhouse and the west section of the quadrangle were destroyed by fire in the 1960s.

J. D. Fletcher's valet, Gray, had the distinction of having his own house built for him, again around 1900, and probably designed by William Flockhart. It would not look out of place in the Home Counties stockbroker belt. It has a mansard roof, unique at Rosehaugh, curious in that the lower slopes are slated and the upper tiled. It seems unlikely that it was designed that way, and the slated roof is probably a repair. An outstanding feature is the massive chimney stack serving a no less impressive inglenook fireplace in the dining room. As Gray was a bachelor and presumably took most of his meals at the Mansion, the kitchen was hopelessly inadequate for a family house, a state of affairs that had to be remedied before it could be occupied by a later married factor (see illustration 101).

J. D. Fletcher's factor, John Henderson, lived in

*98. The Horseshoe Falls.*

*97. The Tower at the Stables (left).*

*99. The main lake. Courtesy of the Brodie of Brodie.*

*100. The Boathouse on the main lake.*

Fortrose, in a house called Canonbury, so it was logical that the Estate Office should also be located there, in the centre of the holdings which by now covered most of the Black Isle. The house designed by Flockhart and built next-door to Canonbury incorporated many of his idiosyncrasies, including a lucarne window and steep roof slopes. Now called Kindeace Lodge, it has been enlarged and converted to a private house, but its lineage is unmistakable (see illustration 105).

The East Lodge, on the road out from Rosehaugh Mains to the village, is now a private dwelling house, as is the West Lodge on the Avoch Road. The West Lodge (see illustration 103) was built by Alexander Ross for James Fletcher, c1870, in an Italianate style with ornate detailing. There is a carriage entrance, whose gates have been removed, and a pedestrian one with cast-iron gates still in place, and all the gate-piers are surmounted with urns.

The other outstanding estate building designed by Flockhart is the Laundry. In common with other large estates at this time all the laundry for the main house was done in a completely separate building. It lies in a remote, unsuspected corner of the policies at the end of a mature lime walk, almost surrounded by trees and poised at the edge of the escarpment overlooking what was once the lake. Architecturally, it is closely related to the Dairy, being in what is called the English Vernacular Revival style, although its walls, instead of coursed stone, are harled and pebble-dashed. It is, in effect, a bungalow with dormers to light the first floor (see illustration 104). The interior walls were all tiled, but we have no idea of the equipment, long since gone.

Another most important area of the estate centred on the horses. The stable block had accommodation for many horses, of which the bloodstock and carriage horses formed the aristocracy; their stables were luxurious, with their harnesses hung in glass fronted cases. A section was set aside for sick horses with two stalls which had a form of central heating. There was also ample space for the four-wheeled brougham, the closed carriage, Victoria

*101. Gray's Cottage, built c1900, William Flockhart, architect.*

102. *The Stables, with additions and alterations by Alexander Ross and William Flockhart.*

103. *West Lodge, Alexander Ross, architect.*

104. *The Laundry, William Flockhart, architect.*

105. *Kindeace, in Fortrose, originally the Estate Office, William Flockhart, architect.*

*106. The Smithy at the Mains Farm.*

and Stanhope phaetons and the eight governess, dog, game and station carts, and in due course, motor cars. The stables were originally designed as a three sided court, and were remodelled by Alexander Ross, James Fletcher's architect, and added to by Flockhart. They are of a more modest style than the Mansion and probably best described as Scottish baronial (see illustration 102). The buildings are now in use as estate workshops. The Stables Cottage provided accommodation for the head coachman.

Rosehaugh Estate had provided shooting for generations of owners, but James Douglas Fletcher decided to extend these considerably. The most fundamental job was to form a boating, fishing and duck shooting lake by building a dam across the Killen Burn. The few families that lived there were re-housed elsewhere to make way for the lake. The dam formed a series of waterfalls, called the Horseshoe Falls, after the shape of the steps. Both this lake and the ornamental lake were stocked with trout. There are several buildings of note in this area.

Firstly, on the main lake, a boathouse. Timber framed on a base of rough random stone, it had a pitched roof covered with the same pink plain tiles as those on the house. The gable-end faced onto the lake and is half-timbered. A balcony, protected by a tiled roof, enclosed three sides of the roughly square building, which consisted at high level, accessible by land, of a single, well-lit room furnished with a handsome stone fireplace. At water level were slipways, moorings and undercover storage for a number of duck punts, canoes and other craft. Since the failure of the dam in 1946, when the retaining wall collapsed and a surge of water six feet high thundered down through Avoch, the boat house remained perched forlornly half-way up the hillside until recent renovation.

Below the Falls stands the Power House, a Tudor style L-shaped building constructed of roughly hewn stone laid to courses, each wing topped with a pyramidical roof

*107. The Power House, William Flockhart, architect.*

*108. The workers' hut on Lime Walk.*

97

*109. The Summerhouse on the Ornamental Lake.*

with a louvred ventilator. Most of the interior wall space was taken up with the switch-gear mounted on marble slabs. There was only one window, interesting as being the only Gothic one specified by Flockhart at Rosehaugh.

On the shore of the ornamental lake below the terraces is a tiny summer house cum boathouse built of timber, covered in ship-lap boards, and having a landing stage at the water's edge. The landing is covered by an extension of the main roof supported on four plain stone columns of vaguely Doric order, although their top sections are octagonal. The building has the air of a Greek temple, enhanced by the use of pantiles for the roof covering. The comfort of the user was, as always at Rosehaugh, given high priority, the interior being provided with a more than adequate stone fireplace.

It would have been quite impossible to house all the estate workers at Rosehaugh itself and many workers came up daily from the village. As was common practice on estates and farms at that time, for those who were provided with accommodation, certain staple foodstuffs: milk, potatoes, turnips, oatmeal; the rent; and some firewood formed part of the wages. The estate was maintained to a very high standard, with all the roads brushed every week. There was a smithy and a sawmill on the Mains Farm and the usual complement of estate carpenters, masons and handymen. On Lime Walk there was a rustic hut built for the use of the estate workers and gardeners. Roads and drives on the estate were constructed so that the inhabitants of the House could walk or drive around without encountering farm or garden traffic. Thus a road was built on the east side of the kitchen garden, passing by means of an underpass and bridge under the East Drive from the house, so that loads of dung and other unsavoury materials could be taken unseen and unsmelt to the garden. Two roads, with bridges over the Rosehaugh Burn, were built out to the railway station from the farm for the transportation of goods.

Day-to-day running of the estate was left in the capable hands of the factor, John Henderson. His father, Alex, had been coachman to Sir J. J. R. MacKenzie and James Fletcher, and his prowess at handling a coach and six in the streets of London was legendary. He later ran a grain store in Fortrose, and his three sons, Alex, Thomas and John were all outstanding businessmen and administrators. John had the distinction of being the longest serving Town Clerk (of Fortrose) in Scotland; he served in this capacity for 75 years and died, in harness, at the age of 96. He was factor at Rosehaugh from 1878 till 1909. On his retirement he was presented with an illuminated address by the tenantry, in the following terms:

*'Presented to Mr John Henderson, late factor, by the tenants of the Rosehaugh Estates as a token of the esteem and respect in which you were held by them for the long period of 32 years. During that time you discharged all the various duties devolving upon you in a most conscientious and straightforward manner between landlord and tenant. In all cases of difficulty your valuable advice was always at our disposal. We trust that in your well-earned retirement you may have that rest which your arduous past duties so richly merit.'*

James Douglas Fletcher's estate at Rosehaugh provided a pleasant and secure haven from which he could pursue his many interests. He was a keen sportsman who created facilities for many of his favourite sports on the estate. He was a public-spirited man who did a great deal to improve living conditions in Avoch and sought to develop farming and commerce on the Black Isle. He had many active business interests and made frequent trips abroad.

His values were the embodiment of the Edwardian era, and he shared with his fellow landowners a blithe confidence that such times would go on forever.

*110. The Kennels Cottage.*

111. *The south side of the quadrangle at the Mains Farm built 1812. Courtesy of the Brodie of Brodie.*

112. *The Bothies to the east of the walled garden.*

113. *The Main Farm, built 1884. Courtesy of K. MacLeman.*

114. *The Slaughterhouse and Cottage.*

115. Colonel Fitzroy Stephen CB of the Rifle Brigade, father
of Lilian Fletcher. Courtesy of John Shaw of Tordarroch.
116. Lilian Stephen. Courtesy of John Shaw of Tordarroch.
117. James Douglas Fletcher wearing a monocle (facing page).

# Chapter 10: The Domestic Scene

JAMES Douglas Fletcher married his cousin, Lilian Maud Augusta Stephen, on 12 January 1909, and when the newly married couple returned after the honeymoon to Rosehaugh the carriage stopped at the West Lodge, where a large crowd of people had gathered to meet them. The horses were unhitched, a stout rope attached and 'a hundred men and lads' pulled the carriage over the crisp snow up the drive towards the House. They were preceded by the children from the local schools, who had all been given a day's holiday and were accompanied by several pipers. Near the House they were joined by the elderly Colin Campbell, a well-known piper in the area, who had composed a special tune for the occasion, *Welcome to your Highland Home*. We are told that the pipers played it 'with great spirit' as they led the way up to the mansion-house. Colin Campbell was an appropriate choice, for, 70 years before, his father had played the pipes at another home-coming: he had been in the service of Sir James Wemyss MacKenzie and had played the pipes to welcome James John Randall MacKenzie and his bride Lady Anne Wentworth Fitzwilliam back to the house, over which they were soon to preside.

James Douglas was 51 when he married, of below average height, inclined to corpulence, with a liking for 'smart' clothes. The tradition was that for the occasion both he and his bride wore red, but whilst we have con-

120. *Violet Hope and Thomas, Rosehaugh 1900. Courtesy of the Brodie of Brodie.*

Brodie was an officer in the Lovat Scouts, and a squadron of Lovat Scouts lined the centre aisle of the church. All the decorations consisted of plants and flowers from the Rosehaugh hothouses. After the reception at Rosehaugh House, the young couple left by motor car – lent for the occasion by Lord Lovat. At night all the tenants were treated to a ceilidh and dance and bonfires were lit all over the estate. In time Violet and Ian Brodie were to have three sons, the youngest of whom, Ninian, after the death of his two elder brothers, became the 25th clan chief from 1943 until his death in 2003.

Lilian and James Douglas Fletcher did not have any children. They shared common interests in outdoor sports, and Mrs Fletcher, though painfully shy, overcame this to take an active part in local affairs. As the Laird's wife she had many duties presiding over local societies and charities. There was much to do in the supervision of the running of such a vast household.

The housekeeper, Miss Bethune, presided over the indoor staff. The housemaids stayed in the house, sleeping in the attic, two to a room, or else came in every day from the village. James Douglas had his own trusted staff, Gray the valet, who had served his father, and John Henderson, his father's factor, though Mr Henderson left office late in 1909. One of the most colourful of all was the chef, Signor Ronzoni. He was a dapper little Italian gentleman, sporting a stiffly waxed moustache, who ruled his domain with a rod of iron. Every morning when he came on duty at eight o'clock, he would expect his kitchens to be scrubbed and the staff immaculately turned out. He was in the habit of taking a weekly walk to the village, when he would dress impeccably in black striped trousers, dark jacket, grey spats, grey homburg hat and carry a silver-topped cane. All this was set off by a pair of gleaming patent leather shoes, although as time went by the effect was somewhat marred by the holes he cut in them in order to relieve his bunions. He always car-

121. Miss Lily Stephen in her pony cart. Courtesy of the Brodie of Brodie.

122. Violet Hope and her ponies, Lady Harriet and Rhona, Rosehaugh 1903. Courtesy of the Brodie of Brodie.

123. 'Seaforth in his motor' with James Douglas Fletcher. Courtesy of the Brodie of Brodie.

124. *James Douglas and his niece, Lilian. Courtesy of John Shaw of Tordarroch.*

ried a paper bag of pan drops in his pocket for distribution to any young villagers he met on his way.

Signor Ronzoni made wonderful meals from the abundant supplies of home-produced ingredients, with the help, in the early years, of several sous-chefs. There were always going to be some items that even the fertile gardens and farms of Rosehaugh would be unable to provide. At the turn of the century Fletcher was buying vintage port for laying down at 31/- a dozen - and ordering 20 to 30 dozen at a time. Larranga Havana cigars at 48/- per hundred were ordered several thousand at a time and cases of Pommery champagne at 144/- a dozen.

It does not come as a surprise that Fletcher was one of the earliest owners of a motor car in the north. In fact, he had several, one of which, being almost certainly the first ever seen in the vicinity of Avoch, caused quite a stir. A contemporary report (about 1900) is worth quoting:

*'I can well remember Fletcher passing us in the first car we ever saw when we were just bairns, all under school age, three families of us. We could hear his car coming before we ever saw it because of the noise it made. We had time to run to the gate and raise our voices as he passed – but never a response from the great man. There he sat, straight as a ramrod at the back, a large basket affair at the side to hold walking sticks or umbrellas, while the chain-driven car rattled on its way. There was a hood to raise if need be but the driver was open to all kinds of weather'.*

We have no information as to the make of this vehicle but it was not long before Fletcher succumbed, as many another rich man after him, to the lure of the Rolls Royce.

This was the even tenor of life at Rosehaugh. There were the grand domestic occasions such as the weddings of Violet Hope and that of James Douglas, there were glittering balls and there were the great national festivities, such as the Coronation of Edward VII, when the whole

*125. Mrs Ethel Elford and her daughter Lilian. Courtesy of John Shaw of Tordarroch.*

village was entertained. In general, life revolved round the shooting season and the London season, when the household decamped to the capital where the Fletchers had a town house. This was a popular break from routine for master and servants alike. For the young women servants to be transported by train from the Highlands to the centre of Mayfair was almost unbearably exciting. Although their financial resources were slim, they would save up in order to savour the delights of the 1d bus rides, 2d bars of Palm toffee, or occasionally, throwing caution to the winds, a cup of tea and a Chelsea bun at Lyons Corner house which cost all of 4d. When the pennies were running low, window shopping was free and Selfridges was a popular mecca. Sometimes a guest would leave a generous tip - even as much as £1, which could open up dazzling prospects. At this time a scullery maid started at an annual wage of £18 with no day off, but three weeks annual holiday, during which she would be given 15/- a week as a contribution to the parental home's house-keeping during her stay. There was a strict hierarchy among the servants, and a scullery-maid, being on one of the lowest rungs, could not speak to any other servant without asking permission. Mr Fletcher had a reputation for being strict, but fair, and appreciated frankness in certain long-serving trusted servants. One keeper, on being asked his opinion of the Airedale newly acquired by the great man commented that 'the best of the dog is the collar it wears'.

The calm order of this world was forever shattered by the outbreak of the war in 1914. Large numbers of the male staff answered the call to arms and the scale of day-to-day existence, as well as that of entertaining had to be curtailed. The Rosehaugh Estate was also able to make an unusual contribution to the war effort. The Lovat Scouts had been formed by Simon Fraser, Lord Lovat, during the Boer War from among the young farmers, stalkers and gamekeepers in the area. During the World War, the Rosehaugh stud provided some ponies for the Scouts. After the Armistice, many retainers who had survived came back and found their positions waiting for them. The Fletchers now had their niece, Lilian Elford, staying with them, daughter of Lilian Fletcher's sister Ethel and her husband John Elford. The little girl grew up surrounded with animals and became an expert horsewoman. Even before she could ride alone, she would accompany her uncle on his rounds of the estate perched on the pommel of his saddle. As she got older, Lilian had a succession of ponies with whom she developed an instinctive rapport, and took four feet jumps without saddle or bridle. She also had a parrot called Greyboy given to her by her aunt when she was five. It lived with her during the rest of her stay at Rosehaugh and went with her on her marriage, living a total of 40 years.

Rosehaugh must have been an idyllic place for the growing child and her presence enlivened family life in the Big House, with Mr Fletcher now approaching 70. Lilian grew into a sensitive, gentle young woman known affectionately by the staff and by local people as Miss B. She endeared herself to all who knew her.

James Douglas had inherited his father's strongly developed sense of social responsibility, and throughout his years at Rosehaugh he used his position and fortune to benefit the local community. No account of his life would be complete without some consideration of his public service.

*126. J.D. Fletcher relaxing in the main porch. Courtesy of the Brodie of Brodie.*

*127. James Douglas Fletcher and John Henderson in front of the Estate Office in Fortrose.*

# Chapter 11: Business, Public Service and Agriculture

AFTER James Fletcher's death in 1885, James Douglas Fletcher, then aged 28, became the laird of Rosehaugh. He took his new responsibilities seriously and, as his father had done before him, he continued to make improvements to Avoch and its surrounds, particularly in water supply and in better sanitation facilities. Pigsties were built to house pigs that had previously roamed freely, and this helped improve hygiene in and around the houses.

In handling the estate he was not only a rich but a progressive landlord, and was helped for a considerable number of years by his outstandingly capable factor, John Henderson. Whenever business affairs took James Douglas away from home, John Henderson would keep him in touch with detailed letters every two or three days. In estate matters, James Douglas relied heavily on Henderson, but his valet Gray was his adviser and confidant in many of his other interests.

James Douglas found the financial world both fascinating and absorbing. He showed financial talent, an ability with figures and was continually aware of current fluctuations in stocks and shares as well as changes in the money markets at home and abroad. These abilities enabled him to make shrewd investments, though this was done not only for monetary gain, but also for the excitement it aroused in him. Many of his stock exchange investments had a bias towards mining, particularly in South Africa, and in 1889 the dealing profit on his mining shares alone was £2335. His cash balances at Liverpool Commercial Banking Co. Ltd., The Bank of Liverpool Ltd. and his brokers H. Moritz, amounted at that time to nearly £70,000. He had other bank accounts and other brokers, so this only gives a flavour of his wealth.

He owned several estates in Ceylon which were used mainly in the production of tea and coffee. With great foresight, he saw possibilities in rubber and bought more estates in Ceylon which gave him rubber sources. After this purchase, he formed a small private company, the Rosehaugh Rubber Company, with John Henderson as secretary, which shortly after was formed into a larger company called the Rosehaugh Tea and Rubber Company, with a capital of one million pounds. There were eventually 2926 acres under tea and 1011 acres under rubber. It is also interesting that he named his private bungalow there 'Fortrose' whilst one of the estates was named 'Culloden' and another 'Rosehaugh'.

Many local people were encouraged to buy shares in the company, which proved to be good advice as the value of

130. *Travels in Africa – 'J.D.F. on the illimitable veldt, a thunderstorm coming on, and broken down.'*

128. *Travels in Africa – 'Going into the drift' – Rhodesia, 1905. All photographs, courtesy of the Brodie of Brodie.*

129. *Travels in Africa – 'Coming out of the drift' – Rhodesia, 1905.*

131. *Travels in Africa – J.D.F. in Nubia, 1901.*

shares rose significantly giving good dividends, until the fall in the price of rubber.

In 1904, he looked at opportunities in Africa and bought an estate in Nelspruit in the Eastern Transvaal which he planned to exploit for its timber potential, although at that time there was not a tree to be seen. He employed the father of the present owner, Mr Hamilton Fowles, as factor of the estate, by now renamed Rosehaugh. By the time James Douglas had sold it to his former factor in 1921, the estate was thriving to such an extent that it had its own railway siding to cope with the timber it was producing. The sale did not mean that James Douglas was abandoning South Africa; he also owned a farm in the Orange Free State, which was still in his possession at the time of his death. Just as his father had done, he was continually exploring new business opportunities. He was generous too in the help he extended to young people in the Black Isle area, giving many the chance of working abroad.

For a number of years, James Douglas was a director of the Highland Railway Company. He felt strongly that easy access to remote parts of the Highlands could be achieved by laying a light narrow gauge railway. During his time as a director, the Black Isle Railway, running from Muir of Ord to Fortrose, was opened and he had his own personal halt at Rosehaugh. In 1895, he caused a stir by questioning some of the financial dealings of Mr Andrew Douglas, then the General Manager of the Highland Railway. As a result Mr Douglas resigned, though he had given many years of loyal service, and James Douglas helped to institute some financial reforms in the company. In 1900, he became chairman of the company for one year after Sir George Macpherson-Grant retired.

In his local area he was a well-known figure and name. He became chairman of the school boards of Avoch and Rosemarkie, and also chairman of Avoch and Rosemarkie Parish Councils. His generosity to local schools with gifts of equipment is well documented. As chairman of the

*132. The Clock Tower at Fortrose Academy,*

School Board, he laid the foundation stone of Fortrose Academy on 30 August 1890, having been granted the freedom of Fortrose earlier that day. The sandstone part of the Academy was finally opened in 1892 with James Douglas donating the clock in the tower (see illustration 132).

In 1854, Alexander George, son of the explorer Sir Alexander MacKenzie and past owner of Avoch Estate, opened the woollen factory in Rose Street in Avoch, naming it Geddes Mill after his mother. Its fortunes fluctuated from the beginning, never reaching commercial viability, and in spite of James Douglas's efforts in forming the Avoch Tweed Mill Company in 1895 with the intention that the proceeds should go to the needy, it finally closed in 1907. He converted the building to 14 accommodation units to help with housing in the area, and these were ready for occupation by 1910. The building no longer stands and in its place, some sheltered housing has been

133. *James Douglas Fletcher at the Rosehaugh Estate, Eastern Transvaal, Africa. Courtesy of the Brodie of Brodie.*

built. As a supporter of the Freemasons, James Douglas gave a room in the Mill as the meeting place for the Freemasons of the area, whose lodge was named 'Lodge Rosehaugh'.

With fishing playing an important part in the Avoch way of life, James Douglas was keen to support the fishermen, particularly in their need for a new harbour. Their existing harbour had been built in 1815 by Sir Alexander MacKenzie. The improvement proposed was to cost £6000, and James Douglas subscribed the sum of £500 towards this venture. He also hosted a three day bazaar at Rosehaugh to help raise funds for this, when 'ladies of some position' in the community each took a stall, and were helped by the local women. Plans were drawn up for a new harbour to be positioned to the west of Avoch, beyond where the Industrial Area is now situated. It was felt that this would provide more shelter for the boats as well as giving deep water. However, after much discussion with the fishermen, it was decided to keep the harbour in its existing position and the money raised was used to extend the harbour facilities.

At county level, he was a Justice of the Peace, Deputy Lieutenant and became vice-convenor of Ross and Cromarty County Council, acting for the convenor, Sir Hector Munro of Fowlis, while Sir Hector was in Egypt with his regiment. Throughout his whole Council connection in his capacity as Avoch councillor, he was chairman of the Black Isle District Committee. His skills as an economist and his views that outlay for a better service was essential but that expenditure should be prudent with no excess or extravagance, made him an ideal chairman of the Finance and General Business Committee. It was suggested that his shrewdness made the Ross-shire rates one of the lowest in the country, while the public services were of the best quality. In 1919, when school boards were replaced by Education Authorities, he became a member but began to question the extravagance of the higher expenditure, though this increase was typical of the post-war era. It is clear from records that he sat on the committees of many other aspects of county life such as the Police Committee, the County Road Board, the Black Isle Farmers' Society, the Black Isle Steam Shipping Company and the Black Isle Combination Poorhouse.

In 1900, he widened his political horizons by standing as the parliamentary candidate for Ross and Cromarty as a Unionist candidate. Unfortunately, at the time of the pre-election campaign, he was unwell and on the advice of his doctor, went to France. This was very much to his disadvantage as he addressed none of the meetings in support of his campaign. It was even suggested that the reason for his absence was that he had been forced into the candidate's position against his wish. In spite of his absence, meetings were held throughout Ross and Cromarty and were attended by district lairds and other influential men well known in the locality. The meetings were well attended by all classes of people and among those who addressed these meetings in James Douglas's support, were well-known local men and two Edinburgh advocates, Mr Orr Deas and Mr Crabbe Watt. It is interesting that Miss Violet Hope is mentioned on several occasions as being present on the platform. James Douglas had made his views known on various issues, and these were put forward in these addresses. At the time, the Boer War was a controversial matter and he made it clear that he was in support of the Government, whose feeling was that the Boer War was inevitable and that everything should be done to stop the Boers gaining control in South Africa. Having travelled extensively in South Africa, James Douglas felt he was in a position to give informed views on this issue. At a local level, he was keen to extend the Crofters Act to those crofters having leasehold. The Crofters Act had given crofters security of tenure and compensation for improvements. This also seemed to be an ideal opportunity to promote again the extension of more light railways in the Highland area, suggesting, amongst others, Garve to Ullapool, Fearn to Portmahomack and Cromarty to Dingwall. It was generally felt that he would make an ideal candidate having lived in the area for most of his life, which made him aware of the needs of the constituents. Unfortunately he lost the election to Mr J. Galloway Weir by 3554 to 1691 votes.

James Fletcher's innovative enthusiasm in agriculture was exceeded by that of his son, who not only built on his father's foundation stock, but also introduced breeds never previously seen in the Highlands. Herds of pedigree beef cattle were reared at different locations on the Estate; Herefords were at Muirhead; Shorthorns remained at Rosehaugh; Aberdeen Angus stock was very successfully bred at Killen Farm. It was from Killen that the formidable British Champion of 1893 came, an Aberdeen Angus heifer 'Pride of the Highlands' of the Cherry Blossom strain. She was described in *Country Gentleman* in January 1894, 'as near perfection as we can possibly expect', and by others as 'magnificently sweet and level, with the greatest quantity of the best quality meat ever seen in a fat heifer'. Pride of the Highlands weighed 17 hundredweight at just under three years, and not only was she Champion of Scotland in 1893 but she also won four of her classes at Smithfield, London in the same year, collecting £1000 prize money for her owner.

Further success was achieved with Shorthorns, though mainly taking place after the death of the Laird. In particular, there was Collynie Royal Leader, bought as a young bull calf by James Douglas Fletcher, and used to improve the stock at Rosehaugh. The bull was shown at the Aberdeen Highland Show in 1928 where, in spite of being placed seventh in his class by an English Judge, his potential was instantly recognised by Captain MacGillivray of Calrossie as being 'the finest beast he had ever seen in a ring', and on hearing that the animal was for sale, Captain MacGillivray immediately contacted Mrs Fletcher and

134. *'The Pride of the Highlands', Smithfield Champion, 1893.*

agreed to purchase Collynie Royal Leader for £2500. His introduction to the Calrossie herd ensured their continuing fame world-wide as top breeders of pedigree Shorthorns, and such was Calrossie's reputation, that a request came from King George V's Estate at Windsor for the use of a pedigree bull. Collynie Royal Leader was despatched on loan to Windsor where he exceeded expectations. Meanwhile he had left a legacy at Rosehaugh, a son 'Rosehaugh Mandarin', which took top prize at the Perth Bull Sales in 1928. Many prize animals at Calrossie carried the blood line of Collynie Royal Leader.

The first herd of Jersey dairy cows in the Highlands arrived on the completion of the Rosehaugh Dairy and these provided a continuous supply of rich milk for the 'Big House' and the immediate Estate. James Douglas's pedigree flock of Black Cheviot Sheep was, at that time, the only one of the breed in the North, though he was also a well-known breeder of Border Leicesters.

The arrival of two West Highland pony mares, Phoenix and Phoenice, from Rhum in 1910, and the purchase of the

*135. King George V with Jock 1935. Courtesy of Royal Collection Trust © Her Majesty Queen Elizabeth II 2016.*

Jock, King George's favourite grey pony, was led, ready saddled, by the chief groom.

*136. Jock at the funeral of George V, 1936.*

impressive and unbeatable stallion 'Glen Bruar' from James MacDonald's stud at Blair Atholl, saw the beginning of a top Highland pony stud at Rosehaugh. The stud's most successful year was 1931, when Lady Phoenix (out of Phoenix by Glen Bruar), one of the finest mares known to the breed, won two championships, a silver medal and the Prince of Wales gold medal, all of them at the Royal Highland and Agricultural Society show in Edinburgh.

Perhaps the most famous Highland pony in the world was Jock, sired by Glen Bruar out of Lady Strathnairn. Jock was sold to King George V, who grew so fond of him that he would ride no other pony. Such was the bond, that at the King's funeral, Jock appeared walking forlornly behind the funeral procession, his saddle empty. This famous pony and his elderly groom, Mr French, retired together but not before Jock was immortalised by the painter Sir Alfred Munnings, who hung the pony's painting at the Munnings exhibition at the Royal Academy.

The Highland ponies had an obvious sporting purpose, but were also much used for general farm work, though the magnificent Clydesdales, of which there was a stud at Suddie, were the champions of work in the fields.

James Douglas was always keen to experiment, be it with crops, such as linseed and flax, or new machinery adapted for use with Rosehaugh's own electrical plant. Despite the extensive and heavy use of lime by his father, which had vastly improved crops, James Douglas sought further improvements in animal feeding and had great success with the introduction of silage. Silo towers were erected at Muiralehouse, Suddie and Killen, with a pit silo being built at Rosehaugh Mains and silage 'choppers' being imported from America as a further experiment.

With such a fine collection of livestock for exhibition, involvement with the many Agricultural Shows was expected, and the Black Isle Show was held at Rosehaugh on many occasions, when the public were permitted to wander freely over the Estate. James Douglas was connected with numerous Agricultural Societies at executive level, such as the Clydesdale, Shetland pony, Border Leicester, Council of Smithfield Show, Royal Highland and Agricultural Society and in 1886, he was president of the Black Isle Farmers' Society, presenting a silver trophy for the Clydesdale competition. Mrs Fletcher continued the tradition and the Black Isle Show was again held at Rosehaugh in 1934, when she provided the use of the marquees.

Throughout his life as owner of Rosehaugh, James Douglas's business acumen and strength of character were undoubted, but, of course, he started his career from the immensely firm base built by his father. He tended to be a shy and aloof man, yet his kind heartedness and generosity, particularly to the local people, are clearly evident in his gifts to them and in the improvements he implemented locally. In his various influential positions, he adhered strictly to his strong principles and ideals. It is hardly surprising that he was well respected by all classes of people throughout the area.

# Chapter 12: Sporting Days

ONCE James Douglas Fletcher had decided to take up an activity, he pursued it with vigour and thoroughness and in no area is this more evident than that of the many sporting facilities with which the estate came to be provided. Field sports - shooting, in particular - were a life-long passion, but, especially in his younger days, J. D. Fletcher was interested in, and an eager exponent of, many different sports, and each one was catered for to a professional standard so that eventually his estate could have played host to a small-scale Olympiad.

Like his father, James Douglas loved cricket – a double legacy no doubt of Lancashire and Moray! He was promoter of the Rosehaugh Cricket Club, of which many prominent local dignitaries in Avoch, Rosemarkie and Fortrose were members. Friends were invited up from the south to play and they used a generous size pitch just north-west of the stables with a fine pavilion. This same field was used at different times of year for other sports, in particular hockey and one match, just weeks before Violet Hope's wedding to Ian Brodie, is very well-recorded, with photographs showing Violet and the younger members of the Brodie family sitting during breaks in the game in cowled wicker chairs and the female members of the party in ankle length divided skirts.

In the coldest parts of the winter James Douglas could indulge a special interest - curling. He built a curling

*137. Shooting luncheon at Rosehaugh. Courtesy of the Brodie of Brodie.*

138. *A hockey match showing J.D. Fletcher and Colonel Stephen, Rosehaugh, 1904. Courtesy of the Brodie of Brodie.*

139. *The same hockey match showing the Pavilion. Courtesy of the Brodie of Brodie.*

140. *James Douglas Fletcher and friends playing croquet. Courtesy of the Brodie of Brodie.*

141. *A game in progress on the curling pond above the boating lake.*

pond on the Killen Burn, above the boating lake (see Ordnance Survey illustration 83 and illustration 141). In 1880 he had founded the Rosehaugh Curling Club, which gained admittance to the Royal Caledonian Curling Club in 1888. There was also a skating pond below the drive to the west of the terraces with an elegant club house, complete with fireplace, and this pond was also used for bonspiels in later years. It was a real frost hollow, where ice sometimes held for weeks, as late as April. James was also a well-known figure in curling circles in the north, especially at Loch-na-Sanais, the well-known curling pond just outside Inverness. A presentation copy of J. Kerr's famous *History of Curling*, with a lengthy inscription from the author to J.D. Fletcher and published in 1890, was among his prized books. The Avoch and Rosemarkie Curling Club presented a very attractive silver-mounted broom to J.D. Fletcher in 1895 and this was returned to the Club after Mrs Fletcher's death. It has been competed for a number of times since 1954.

Typical country house pursuits for the summer months were tennis and croquet. There were fine new tennis courts laid out below the terraces and to the east of the house, and our photograph (see illustration 140) shows an elegantly dressed James Douglas playing croquet with some friends on the lawn.

In 1888 Fletcher became patron of the Fortrose and Rosemarkie Golf Club, then in its formative years, and he feued, free of charge, some of the land over which members play to this day. He owned a summer bungalow behind the ladies' tee of the 482 yard sixth hole still appropriately called 'Rosehaugh'. His future wife, Lilian Stephen, and her family were very keen golfers - Lilian won the Silver Medal in 1895 and 1896 and the Silver Cup in 1896. James Douglas himself does not appear to have played particularly often, probably confining his efforts in this direction to the practice holes on the estate, although he did take his friend Andrew Carnegie out to play at Fortrose: Carnegie and his party would sail down by yacht from Skibo Castle near Dornoch, anchor in the Firth and come ashore to play a few holes. Our photograph (see illustration 143) shows the family having a picnic lunch at the summer bungalow – then a simple wooden structure with a tin roof, and still standing, though now faced and re-roofed. J.D. Fletcher donated a medal to the Club in 1890. Known as the Rosehaugh Medal, it is still played for and is one of the most coveted at the Club.

There are no records of J.D. Fletcher playing soccer, but shortly after Inverness Thistle Football Club was formed in 1885, he became one of its patrons.

Riding and driving carriage horses were not just pastimes in those days, but essential activities in the time before the internal combustion engine. We have already seen that the accommodation provided for the thoroughbred horses was luxurious. Even more ambitious was the laying-out of a seven-furlong race track which was soon nick-named Little Ascot by the locals. A few race meetings were held there, along the lines of the better-known pony races at Dunain near Inverness, but principally the course was used to train and exhibit the horses bred on the estate. Most famous of all the horses, was the Rosehaugh stud of Highland Ponies.

The activity around which much of the life of the estate revolved and the one nearest to J.D. Fletcher's heart, was shooting and other field sports, such as stalking and fishing. We have already seen how earlier in the 19th century James John Randall MacKenzie had extended and improved the buildings on the estate with new kennels and keepers' cottages. Some rough shooting for the laird and a few friends was always an essential part of the country life but towards the end of the century, with the omnipresent and enthusiastic example of the Prince of Wales, later Edward VII, shooting was to become much more organised on most of the large estates. Huge numbers of game-birds were reared, small armies of keepers,

142. *Violet Hope at the presentation of a trophy in front of the Fletchers' bungalow on the golf course.*

143. *Summer luncheon on the golf course, the Fletcher's bungalow at the sixth tee. Photographs courtesy of the Brodie of Brodie.*

beaters and loaders employed and the whole social scene centred for months on end round the large shooting parties. Rosehaugh was no exception. Up to a dozen keepers and foresters worked under a head keeper and during the season large parties arrived to enjoy the sport, among whom were Lord Burton, H.J. Gladstone (son of William), William Cunard and Andrew Carnegie.

We have a photograph of a shooting luncheon en plein air presided over by J.D. Fletcher, complete with piper, and others of a similar occasion at Auchterflow in October 1901 (see illustrations 137 and 144). Once the re-organisation of the shooting was in full swing, bags increased, and a page from the Game Book in 1900 shows the great variety of birds shot on four days in November (see illustration 146). The head gamekeeper at this time was called Dinwoodie. His photograph with his wife and young family in front of the kennels cottage is shown in illustration 145. He was presented with a pair of Purdey guns by James Douglas Fletcher for all his years of service. William Whyte, taken on as a very young man in 1924, recalled that at that time nine keepers worked on the estate. He was not provided with tweeds, but received a double barrel shotgun. He was paid £1 a week. 3000 pheasants were reared for Rosehaugh alone, and among Whyte's other duties was the care of the spaniels and labradors kept for sport. The keepers were kept busy trapping and controlling vermin and keeping a weather eye open for local poachers.

However good the shooting was at Rosehaugh, there were not, on the Black Isle, the open moors needed for grouse and red deer. To fill this gap, J.D. Fletcher bought a sporting moor near Kingussie and built the shooting lodge of Pitmain near the shores of Loch Gynack, during the years of the First World War (see illustrations 148 and 149). There was fine craftsmanship in the building of the house, a private power house for electricity and a walled garden producing all sorts of vegetables and fruit, all

grown to come into season just as the shooting parties arrived. Every year, in good time for the 'Glorious 12th' of August, almost the entire household at Rosehaugh upped sticks and set out for the grouse moors. This exodus was known as the 'Big Trek': the vanguard consisted of a vast shooting brake holding up to 10 people; then by train from Rosehaugh to Kingussie, came the rest of the household: keepers, servants and the dogs, horses, pigs, hens and Jersey cows. The shooters spent several weeks there, returning to Rosehaugh for the autumn pheasant shoots. The year 1927 was an excellent one for grouse, and Fletcher's party at Pitmain was enjoying good sport, when about the 28 August, Fletcher complained of feeling unwell. He suffered a severe heart attack, and was taken back to his beloved Rosehaugh. He died there three days later. His funeral was private.

Apart from several bequests, James Douglas Fletcher left the bulk of his estate to his wife. For the long years of widowhood that lay ahead, Lilian Fletcher was to be in sole charge at Rosehaugh.

*144. Shooting luncheon at Auchterflow. Courtesy of the Brodie of Brodie.*

145. Dinwoodie, the head game-keeper and his family at the Kennels Cottage. Courtesy of Mrs Stephen.

| | Pheasants. | | Partridges | Woodcock | Wild Duck | Hares | Rabbits | Vermin | Totals. |
|---|---|---|---|---|---|---|---|---|---|
| | Cocks. | Hens. | | | | | | | |
| w. 1st | Suddie | 180 | 126 | 7 | 4 | 5 | 36 | 10 | 24 | 392 |
| 2nd | Tourie Lum | 116 | 151 | 21 | | | 44 | 6 | 7 | 345 |
| 3rd | Rosehaugh | 210 | 151 | 7 | 1 | 6 | 24 | 4 | 24 | 427 |
| 5th | Auoch | 39 | 16 | 10 | 1 | 23 | 17 | 60 | 3 | 162 |

146. Page from the Game Book, 1900. Courtesy of the Brodie of Brodie.

147. *Staff, including keepers and beaters, at Rosehaugh.*

148. *Shooting Lodge at Pitmain. Courtesy of John Shaw of Tordarroch.*

149. *James Douglas Fletcher and friend at Pitmain. Courtesy of John Shaw of Tordarroch.*

# Chapter 13: The Final Years

AFTER the death of James Douglas Fletcher, his widow Lilian decided to commission a memorial and burial place on the estate, rather than have her husband interred in the family vault in the Churchyard at the Parish Church in Avoch. She no doubt felt that Rosehaugh was the most fitting place for the burial of the man who had devoted so much of his life to the estate. The architect chosen to design this burial enclosure in 1928 was the very eminent Sir Edwin Lutyens (1869 - 1944). We have already seen how the careers of Lutyens and William Flockhart had touched at several points. They both studied at the Kensington School of Art, though at different times, and otherwise followed quite different career paths. Lutyens had been a frail child and received little in the way of formal schooling. He always maintained that this gave him the opportunity to think for himself. He did not finish his studies at the Kensington School of Art, as he felt there was no more to be learnt there. He clearly showed talent, and influential friends gave him the opportunity to rise quickly as an architect. His work was diverse and not confined to Britain. A list of his many works include memorials, tombs and houses in countries as far apart as the USA, Australia, South Africa, Spain, Italy and France. In particular, he designed both the exterior and interior of many important buildings in New Delhi, India, one of the most elaborate being the Viceroy's home.

*150. The cross in place at the entrance to the Fletchers' burial enclosure at Rosehaugh, 1928. Sir Edwin Lutyens RA, architect. Courtesy of K. MacLean.*

*151. The enclosure at Rosehaugh, 1928. Courtesy of K. MacLean.*

In Britain itself, some of his well-known works show clearly the breadth of his talent. These include Lindisfarne Castle, 1902, the Cenotaph at Whitehall in London, 1919, Queen Mary's Dolls' House, now housed at Windsor Castle, 1920, and Liverpool R. C. Cathedral, 1929. However records of his work show that he was also commissioned to design many private memorials, including one at Dunrobin Castle, in Sutherland.

The burial enclosure for the Fletchers is positioned to the north of where the Rosehaugh greenhouses were situated. It is circular, with a heavy stone balustrade which has a continuous stone bench seat on the inside wall. The balustrade is broken by the entrance gate, and diametrically opposite is an oblong stone bearing a circular plaque on which is the inscription: 'JAMES DOUGLAS FLETCHER AUGUST 30 1927 AND LILIAN MAUD AUGUSTA STEPHEN OCTOBER 30 1953'. To the right and left of the circular plaque, simple laurel garlands are draped. On the back of the stone on the outside of the enclosure is the inscription 'SIR EDWIN L LUTYENS RA. INVT'. The bronze gates themselves are plain, but, above them, supported by the square stone pillars on either side, is a

*152. The burial enclosure today.*

131

bronze arch which carries the initials J. D. and L. F. intertwined with roses. This is not contemporary with the enclosure, and the quality is not what one would expect from the hand of Lutyens. In the centre of the enclosure, a stone cross lies flat on the ground. This cross had originally stood vertically on a flat circular stone guarding the entrance, its arms resting on the piers, but was replaced by the gates and arch, after Lilian Fletcher's death. The circular stone base, however, may still be seen on entering the enclosure. This area is overgrown, and the previously white stone is badly discoloured. For some years, no obvious path to the memorial was in evidence, and for someone not familiar with the area it was difficult to find, as the perimeter fence had been flattened by many years of continuous encroachment by shooters and beaters in pursuit of pheasants. It was sad that the work of such a fine architect and the final resting place of the last Laird of Rosehaugh and his lady should be so badly neglected. However, after the whole of the site that housed the grave area was sold to the estate's present owner, a path was cleared to the grave and the avenue of blue cedar trees, that once lined the path, is now in evidence.

Lilian Maud Augusta outlived her husband by 26 years, and the period of the 1930s and 1940s were not easy ones for the country as a whole, still less for the large country house and estate, whose time, in retrospect, had passed. For the first few years, Mrs Fletcher continued to maintain her house much as it had always been and to hold charity events, such as a sale in 1935 to raise money for the Nursing Association. Children's treats were also held at Rosehaugh. Mrs Fletcher's niece, Lilian Elford, continued to live there, and there were some glittering occasions such as her coming-of-age, when there was a great ball, as well as a presentation from the tenantry on the estate, made by the oldest tenant, Mrs Betsy Jack, resplendent in a snow-white mutch. There was general rejoicing when it was announced that Miss Elford was to

*153. Presentation to Lilian Elford by Mrs Betsy Jack.*

marry Captain Charles John Shaw-MacKenzie of the neighbouring estate of Newhall on the north side of the Black Isle. John Henderson, now well over 80, proposed the toast at their wedding in 1933 on behalf of everyone on the estate.

There had been considerable anxiety on the estate and among the tenant farmers at the prospect of control passing to Mrs Fletcher, but this subsided as she proved to have a skilful combination of fairness and firmness, well able to take intelligent and rational decisions. She had the advice of various factors, but left no-one in doubt that she was the ultimate authority. In the years following the First War most of the sports had been abandoned, leaving only the shooting and the fishing. Mrs Fletcher now made con-

*154. Miss Lilian Elford at Rosehaugh, courtesy of John Shaw of Tordarroch.*

To Investors

## ROSS AND CROMARTY
### ON THE BLACK ISLE

Inverness 10 miles        Dingwall 14 miles

One of the Finest Agricultural Investments
in the Kingdom

# The Estate of Rosehaugh
### (Vale of Roses)

## ROSS-SHIRE

Renowned for its high standard of farming and warm, natural fertility,
a property extending to approximately

### 8,100 ACRES

and including 43 Farms, many Feus, Site Rents, and other Property comprised in
the Township of Avoch, and the valuable Salmon Fishing and Netting Rights
in the Moray Firth at Ethie. The whole producing an annual and
estimated rental of approximately

### £6,300 per annum

To be offered for SALE BY AUCTION, first as a whole, and if not so sold
then in Three Lots, viz.—

LOT 1—The Lands of Suddie, Auchterflow, Killen and others to the North and
East of the Estate extending to approximately 3,300 Acres, and producing
an actual and estimated rental of approximately £2,600 per annum.

LOT 2—Avoch Town Feus, Long Leases, Site Rents, and other property, with
the Farms of Muirelehouse, Craiglands, Bennetsfield, and others to the
South and along the sea board, in all about 3,200 Acres producing an
actual and estimated rental of approximately £3,000 per annum.

LOT 3—The valuable Salmon Fishing Rights in the Moray Firth at Ethie
together with the mains of Ethie and other Farms extending in all to 1,600
Acres, and producing an actual and estimated rental of approximately
£700 per annum, by

## Messrs. JACKSON STOPS AND STAFF

### At the CALEDONIAN HOTEL, EDINBURGH
## On Tuesday, the 29th June, 1943
at 3 p.m.

Solicitors : Messrs. KENNETH BROWN BAKER BAKER, Essex House, Essex Street,
Strand, W.C. 2 (Tel. Temple Bar 2871)
Messrs. STEEDMAN RAMAGE & CO., 6, Alva Street, Edinburgh (Tel. 22273)

Auctioneers : Messrs. JACKSON STOPS & STAFF, 15, Bond Street, Leeds 1 (Tel. 31269)
Also at London, Northampton, Cirencester, Yeovil, Dublin, etc.

Arthur Wigley & Sons Ltd. The Waverley Press, Leeds 6

155. Captain Charles John Shaw-MacKenzie of Newhall and Miss Lilian Elford on their wedding day at Rosehaugh in 1933. Courtesy of John Shaw of Tordarroch.

156. Front cover of the sale catalogue of 1943, Jackson, Stops and Staff.

siderable reductions in the game-keeping staff and the annual trips to Pitmain ceased. The Lodge was used by the Army during World War Two, and, in a sadly deteriorated condition, was demolished in the Fifties.

Mrs Fletcher had also brought back into cultivation large areas of permanent pasture previously left untilled. She took over the management of this large estate at a difficult time for British agriculture. The world slump had been matched by falling cereal prices, which reached their lowest around 1932. At this time it was not unknown for grain to be dumped, and animals, which could not be sold, to be shot by farmers unable to feed them. The rich lands of the Black Isle, and the fact that the Rosehaugh farms had been improved over the years of the Fletchers' ownership, meant that Mrs Fletcher's tenants were to some extent cushioned from the worst effects of the agricultural depression, but nevertheless in the six years from 1928 to 1934 10 farms – Craiglands, Killen, Raddery, The Bog, Wester and Easter Auchterflow, Strath, Upper Raddery, Templand, Drum – were vacated, and there was considerable difficulty in finding new tenants. Hard times can lead to fractious arguments and the manner of some of her factors did little to smooth matters over, but Mrs Fletcher was shrewd enough to bring in other trusted tenant farmers to mediate in awkward situations and her intelligent and pragmatic approach usually resolved the problem.

Nevertheless, running the estate must have been a daunting task for a lady approaching 70, and in June 1943 Jackson, Stops and Staffs advertised the sale of the Rosehaugh Estate to be held at the Caledonian Hotel, Edinburgh; only the House, Policies and the Mains Farm were excepted. It can hardly have been an ideal time to sell off such a large area of prime land, with the country in the middle of a war which could have gone on indefinitely. In the event, the estate was withdrawn from sale, and, at the end of the war a private sale was made, to the Marquis of Bute. Later the farms were sold to the Kilcoy Estates, and these passed, in turn, into the hands of the Eagle Star Insurance Company.

During the years of the Depression, Mrs Fletcher continued charity work, and in 1934, the United Free Church ceased to be used as a church and reverted to Mrs Fletcher as landlord: she gave it to the village for use as a Hall. The number of Mrs Fletcher's private staff fell continuously, until she was surrounded only by a small number of long-serving faithfuls. Alick Matheson was her chauffeur; John MacDonald was an estate worker, who continued to tend the burial enclosure until his own death; Ronzoni, the chef, had been there as long as anyone, and after his death in January 1952, a cook came in from the village. Mrs Fletcher is remembered as a remote and dignified figure, and one can only admire the strength of character it must have taken to live on almost alone in the great house. She died in October 1953 and was buried alongside her husband on the estate. As a final act the cross which had stood at the entrance for 25 years was laid over the graves, and the bronze gate put up in its place.

The house, its contents, policies and the home farm were left to Mrs Fletcher's niece, Mrs Shaw-MacKenzie of Newhall. Mrs Shaw-MacKenzie, and her husband, a distinguished soldier, became known as Major and Mrs Shaw of Tordarroch in 1957, as he assumed his place as 16th hereditary chief of Clan Ay of Tordarroch and 21st Chief of Clan Shaw. They donated several items from the house, in particular the great figure of the Buddha which stood on the terraces, and a pair of magnificent bronze temple lanterns to the Royal Scottish Museum in Chambers Street, Edinburgh, and a number of items were also presented to the village. At a time of national austerity, it was difficult to imagine what could be done with the house, which by now needed extensive and costly repairs. Within a short time everything was sold to the Eagle Star Insurance Company, lock, stock and barrel.

Rosehaugh

AVOCH, ROSS-SHIRE.

CATALOGUE

OF

The Contents

OF

The Mansion House of Rosehaugh

TO BE SOLD BY AUCTION ON THE PREMISES

BY

Messrs. THOMAS LOVE & SONS

Illustrated Catalogues - - - 5/- each

*From*

JAMES W. KING, Esq.,
*Estate Agent,*
8 Charlotte Street,
PERTH.
'Phone: Perth 1778.

Messrs. THOS. LOVE & SONS,
St. John's Place,
PERTH.
'Phones: Perth 2226 (3 lines).
'Grams: "Loves, Perth."

ANDREW WALLACE, Esq.,
*Estate Factor,*
AVOCH,
Ross-shire.
'Phone: Fortrose 349.

**Note.**—The MANSION HOUSE is for SALE.
*Particulars from* JAMES W. KING, Esq.

*157. Crowds at Rosehaugh for the sale in 1954
by Thomas Love & Son, Perth.*

136

# Chapter 14: The Sale and Demolition

WITHIN months of acquiring ownership of Rosehaugh, the Eagle Star Insurance Company proceeded to release some of the capital invested by selling the contents of the House.

It was the largest event ever staged on the Black Isle – an eight day sale, on the premises, organised by Thomas Love & Sons of Perth, though, prior to this, rare and valuable artefacts had been removed from the House and sold in London. Love & Sons produced an illustrated catalogue which cost 5/- in times when a weekly wage for many was £3, resulting in one catalogue passing through several hands, in people's determination not to miss the opportunity of viewing what remained of the Fletcher wealth. Fervent interest and curiosity were aroused far and wide by this extraordinary house sale.

It took place in 1954 from Monday 23 August to Friday 27 August, and Tuesday 31 August to Thursday 2 September, beginning each day at 11 a.m. with the contents on view from Thursday 19 to Saturday 21 August. During these days the excitement increased. In the mornings there was a constant stream of all modes of transport towards Rosehaugh. They came by motor-car, by bicycle and on foot.

The Kessock Bridge was not in existence then and the boat on the Kessock Ferry simply could not hope to transport the volume of traffic from the South, thus leaving the frustrated to make the 26 mile journey round the

*158. James Douglas Fletcher's red Rolls Royce, 1910, JS 191. Courtesy of Sotheby's.*

Firth by Beauly. In two days 700 vehicles are reported to have made the crossing.

The catalogue listed 1984 lots. However, that did not include the large quantity of household napery, nor the vast quantity of furniture and furnishings of lesser importance, nor the contents of the stables and out-hous-

159. Some of the carriages lined up in front of the stables. Courtesy K. MacLean.

160. The French mantelpiece set by Kinable, Lot 572. Price realised £310.

161. One of the pair of bronze elephants 'as big as ponies', Lot 49. Price realised for the pair £90.

es. It is perhaps significant that even the auctioneers were unsure of the pace of the Sale when they printed in the catalogue 'Wed. 1st Sept – and the following day if necessary.' Potential bidders came from all parts and all walks of life, consisting of dealers, gentry, the farming fraternity, city and town dwellers and local inhabitants. The chief auctioneer, Mr James Slater, was indeed faced with a formidable task.

Day One commenced on the terracing where garden ornaments, seats and a variety of damaged goods were disposed of. Among the most notable of the first day were a unique and valuable French stone oval fountain head (£90) and a pair of large heavy bronze Ceylonese elephants (£90). The bronze Burmese chindits which guarded the front door were bought for a New Orleans antiques firm at £56.

The Sale transferred indoors to the Main Hall where prices fluctuated from 2/- for a rubber door mat to the top price of the day - £405 for the Indian carpet which covered the hall floor and measured 49 feet by 21 feet 10 inches (see illustrations 36 and 38). Such was the excitement amongst the throng that the auctioneer had to call frequently for silence as the bidding could not be heard.

On Day Two the contents of the Morning Room, Drawing Room and the East ground floor were dealt with. Prices remained high for outstanding antique articles such as a valuable French mantelpiece set by Kinable (£310) (see illustration 160) and a French kingwood display cabinet which achieved the top price of the day at £400. On the same day a pair of six feet long white cotton curtains made 1/- and the oddity of the Sale was a miniature skeleton under glass, part of a collection of archaeological specimens. Though the Gun Room was included in this day's itinerary no firearms were sold.

The disposing of the library occupied the whole of Day Three and was certainly a day for specialists. Rosehaugh had housed a very fine private library of books. James Douglas often took extracts for his many after-dinner speeches from the large selection of signed first editions by Oscar Wilde. Six lots contained books and material concerning the lives of highwaymen and, of these lots, the most fascinating was a collection of original newspaper cuttings (1735-39) relating to Dick Turpin. The library contained many of the books typical of the country-house library of the day: fine bound sets, plate books on natural history, sporting books and books on local history, many of them in specially commissioned fine leather bindings. Jack Joseph, the London bookseller, paid £1063 for his purchases which included a valuable single volume: Mary Lawrance's *Collection of Roses from Nature* for which he paid £410.

The most affluent buyers had abandoned the Sale by the fourth day and prices settled at more realistic and affordable levels. On this and the following day the contents of the first and second floor bedrooms were sold, clearly displaying the decline of the great House with damaged bedroom sets and faded curtains and furniture. In spite of this the bidding continued briskly.

On the remaining days, large quantities of table and household linen and kitchen utensils were cleared. Much of the linen was embroidered with Rosehaugh or an 'R' and it was appropriate that a large amount of it went to local buyers. James Douglas had commissioned a large selection of personalised table crystal, bearing his crest and initials. It was of an extremely delicate quality which resulted in a regrettable depletion through breakages. A small selection of this crystal sold for £17.

The farming community and estate owners were the main buyers on the last day when the horse-drawn coaches and pony traps were sold. There was, however, an astute buyer from Fife. Mr Kerr from Culross interrupted his holiday in order to purchase five of the carriages with the intention of hiring them to customers for special occasions. Though many of the horse-drawn con-

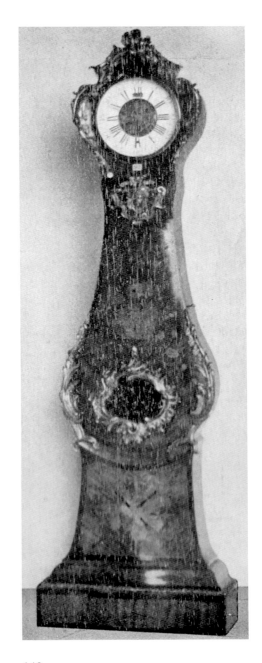

162. *French Salon Clock, movement by Robert, Paris. Lot 563. Price realised £305.*

163. *Chinese Porcelain Jar. Lot 117. Price realised £17.*

164. *Pair of Old Glass Open-work Jars and Pair of Bowls on Stems. Lot 667. Price realised £23.*

*165. French Kingwood and Marqueterie Writing Desk. Lot 525. Price realised £72. (Above, left)*

*166. Brass Regency Clock by Boudet, Paris and Pair of Bronze and Ormulo Gilt Eagle Three-light Candelabra on a Louis XV Kingwood Writing Table. Lots 524 & 669. Price realised by clock and candelabra £56.*

*167. Satinwood and Marqueterie Lady's Secretaire. Lot 533. Price realised £52. (Right)*

*168. Mahogany Writing Cabinet. Lot 590.*

169. Cast Iron Fire Back Plate with the Royal Arms Design. Lot 100. Price realised £38.

170. Late 16th to early 17th Century German Stained Glass Panel in rich colours of yellow, red and blue. Lot 604.

171. One of 112 Plates from an Old Spode Dinner Service. Lot 1391. Price realised for complete service £145.

172. *Louis XVI French Salon Suite Carved and Gilt Wood Fauteuil. Lot 632. (Above)*

173. *Stuart Walnut Dining Chairs. Lot 192. Price realised for the set £31. (Above, right)*

174. *Mahogany Dining Chairs of Chippendale design. Lot 148. Price realised £8 15/- each. (Right)*

veyances were still in good condition, in spite of being 50 years old, their limited appeal was reflected in the prices which varied from £1 to £15.

The sale catalogue made no mention of the two Rolls-Royce cars known to have been garaged in the stables and coach house. One was a sleek modern model but the other was of particular interest. It was a Silver Ghost 40/50H.P., a double Pullman limousine and had been ordered by James Douglas Fletcher in 1910. Reports said that the car had been taken to America but on 1 July 1991, Sotheby's displayed the car – JS 191 – in their sale catalogue. Enquiries revealed that it had been withdrawn at £65,000. It is one of the few surviving models to retain its original coachwork by S. & A. Fuller of Bath (see illustration 158).

It must have been with great relief that Mr James Salter brought the gavel down on the final lot.

Once the furnishings had been removed many rumours abounded as to the fate of the house. Eagle Star was interested in selling, but a house of such proportions had a limited market and the roof required major repairs to some of the main beams. The roof damage has not been attributed to one single cause, but, instead, to a combination of different roofing techniques employed by the builders, the non-traditional use of clay tiles as opposed to slate and the lack of adequate maintenance.

Unconfirmed rumours had it that the Queen Mother and Gordonstoun School had been prospective buyers. No substance has been given to such rumours but what has been confirmed is that the representatives of Butlin's Camps gave the house and grounds serious consideration. They carried out extensive surveys on the area and house, but the immense cost of repairs, rewiring and alterations decided them against it.

With no conclusive sale in prospect, Eagle Star took the irreversible decision in 1958 to demolish the House, and Love & Sons of Perth acting in conjunction with Henry Spencer & Sons of Nottinghamshire were employed to organise the sale of fine fixtures and fittings. The illustrated catalogue cost 2/6d and had allowances made for up to 325 lots. This, the first of a series of demolition sales, had viewing available for six days with the Sale beginning at 11 a.m. on Thursday 21 May 1959 with the added proviso that all lots purchased be removed by 4pm on Thursday 4 June.

The curious, the interested and the determined flocked once again to Rosehaugh though, on this occasion, not in such voluminous numbers as in 1954. The buyers were mainly dealers or those in the construction business and trades. A prominent local buyer was Mr William Logan, Dingwall, whose Muir of Ord based company constructed many of the hydro-electric dams, tunnels and roads.

The major buyer of the day was Mr John Beadle, an antique dealer from Hounslow, London, whose purchases were destined for America and the Continent. He acquired the entire fittings of the most lavish room of all, the Dining Room, with the exception of the fireplace and floor, for £195. The lot had comprised three chandeliers, imposing entrance doors, two smaller doors with a ceiling to match, gilded panelling and Italian cut-velvet wall panels. The auctioneer had anticipated a price of over £1000.

Mr Beadle had similar success in the Louis XVI Drawing Room where the complete gilded panelling and doors became his for £400 with the French veined-marble mantelpiece, destined for a customer in Milan, costing him £205. The oak strip suspended ballroom floor, 1456 square feet, sold for £140 but the selling price of the Grand Hall's brass chandeliers which were each five feet in diameter with six scrolled branches is unknown. £180 was paid for the main staircase of chestnut wood treads, an elaborate wrought-iron balustrade and a moulded brass handrail.

Several local business men featured as buyers with one

*175. The demolition: 1959, the remains of the tower (above) and the front of the house.*

of them purchasing a large amount of panelling, fireplace tiles, windows and flooring, all of which were incorporated in a new house built in Inverness and designed to accommodate the Rosehaugh purchases.

A near disaster occurred when one of the largest fireplaces began its long journey south at Avoch Railway Station. The weight of the fireplace was considerable and the condition of the Black Isle Railway wagon none too reliable, resulting in the disintegration of the wagon floor with the fireplace settling finally on the railway line. Two other fireplaces are suitably displayed in the Portland Arms Hotel, Lybster, where they are regularly used in the winter.

The marble fittings from the Swimming Pool and Turkish Baths were bought by Mr William Logan at £60 and £30 respectively and, along with a quantity of flooring, were to be used in his new headquarter offices at Muir of Ord. The windows, lead guttering, carved stones

and balustrades were sold at a later sale in June 1959 and many a house in the Highlands can boast a window from Rosehaugh.

The task of demolition was allotted to Thomas Oakley of Luton, Bedfordshire, and though most of the workforce came with the firm, several local men were employed. Mr William Logan bought much of the facing stone, transporting some of it to his hydro-electric projects in Wales, while retaining the remainder for his new house which was built at the bottom of Kinnairdie Avenue, Dingwall. The more ornate stones were removed for Mr Logan by his own men and taken to his depot at Muir of Ord where several suffered accidental damage at a later date from a mechanical digger. The house which can be seen above the football-pitch in the village of

145

*176. The demolition: 1959, view from the west.*

*177. A group viewing the west façade.*

*178. Nature returns – the top of the terraces, 1996.*

Avoch was also built entirely of Rosehaugh stone by local councillor and farmer, A. J. Mann.

By 12 July 1959, the house was virtually demolished but the proud 120-foot-high tower still remained. Two I. C. I. experts arrived to take control of its destruction by dynamite. On Wednesday 25 August, as the Avoch children finished their morning break at school the teachers joined them in the playground and all eyes turned west to the trees at Rosehaugh where the tower stood defiantly. At 11 am precisely a loud boom was heard and the tower slid gracefully from view. The landmark, marvelled at by many from the Avoch-Munlochy road, had gone forever.

The firm of Thomas Oakley lost £3000 on the project as the stone which they had expected to sell proved too expensive to extract intact. The unsold stone, much of it beautifully chiselled, was tipped reluctantly back into the quarry. The demolition was completed by 29 September and the site finally levelled on 15 October 1959.

The history of the house was at an end but the life of the Estate and the policies went on. Eagle Star continued as owner of the Rosehaugh and Kilcoy Estates with James King, Perth, and later Bidwells and King, acting as Scottish agents and they, in turn, were represented at local level by factors. Public access to Rosehaugh became increasingly difficult with periodic attempts being made to prevent use of rights of way. It was not possible to wander through the remains of the Gardens and visitors and walkers alike were challenged or turned back. These restrictions resulted largely from the relatively successful poaching of the Estate pheasants reared annually for organised shoots. Access was acceptable if on business or by prior arrangement.

An amalgamation of Eagle Star with British American Tobacco Industries led to a reorganisation of their commercial interests and in 1991 Rosehaugh and Kilcoy Estates were offered for sale. A local farmers' combined

*179. The site of the House in 1996.*

*190. The wine cellars – the only remaining part of the house.*

offer was unacceptable, and Broadland Properties Ltd., Scarborough became the new owners, with Cluttons of Edinburgh being their Scottish representatives.

*191. Aerial view showing the Boathouse on the right and The Power House on the left with the new dam and pathways. The barrier on the left of the lake is the original dam wall and the Horse Shoe Falls can be seen flowing down from the lake towards The Power House. Courtesy of Broadland Properties.*

# Chapter 15: Rosehaugh Estate Now

TWO hundred years ago Sir Roderick MacKenzie had just moved his family into his 'new and commodious' mansion house at Rosehaugh. A century later James Douglas Fletcher was embarking on an ambitious scheme to transform this house into a fairytale confection, complete with every comfort money could buy. Woolton Hill House in Liverpool, Dale Park in Sussex, Pitmain Lodge near Kingussie, Rosehaugh House: they all fell victim, one after the other, in the space of a few years, to the ravages of time and the austerity of the postwar era. Only one of the grand houses that belonged to the Fletchers still stands, Letham Grange in Forfar, and it is no longer a private residence. But time did not stand still on the Rosehaugh Estate.

The former Estates of Rosehaugh and Kilcoy, purchased by Broadland Properties Ltd. from The Eagle Star Insurance Company in 1991, extended to some 14,500 acres. These are some of the changes and improvements, which have been made to the Estate in the last 25 years.

Firstly, the new owners rationalized the management of the Estate by allowing most of the tenants of the outlying farms to purchase their farms. They also sold land for housing development at Avoch, Munlochy and North Kessock, thereby providing much needed new residential housing for the area. They cleared the trees on the Ormond Castle Mound to allow better public access to this historic site. They have sold some of the less productive Forestry Plantations including the Craig Wood between Avoch and Fortrose and the Plantations along the cliffs at Eathie. Rosehaugh Estate now extends to some 4000 acres, which is actively managed on behalf of the owners by Peter Graham and Associates. Much of the existing Forestry has been replanted, and two of the farms, on which the former tenants have now retired, are being farmed in-hand. Two new cottages have been built at Bennetsfield and Corrachie, and are now let as residential properties. All the other occupied houses on the Estate have been renovated.

One of the features of the Estate was the large Boating Lake, which had been created by building a dam across the Killen Burn. After the dam was breached in 1946, this large lake disappeared, and trees replaced the water. A much smaller lake has now been created beside the former Boathouse using part of the original dam wall, and water flows over the Horse Shoe Falls again (see illustration 191). The ornamental lake below the Terraces has also been drained and refilled and the Summer House beside it has been restored to its former glory (see illustrations 109 and 195). Providing signposts for footpaths and a small car park at the main entrance now encourages public access over much of the Estate.

The farm buildings at Bay Farm were no longer being used for farming, and in 2000 it was decided to convert these buildings into holiday cottages. It was originally

192. *The renovated Boathouse. Courtesy of Broadland Properties.*

193. *The Boathouse before renovation. Courtesy of Broadland Properties.*

intended to use the existing structure, but this did not prove practicable. During the demolition of the old stone walls, an interesting reminder of their former use came to light when an unexploded hand grenade was discovered in the rubble. The previous tenant of the farm had been the Captain of the local Home Guard during World War II, and had obviously stored grenades there. The Police were called at once and all work had to be stopped until the Bomb Disposal Squad had been summoned from Edinburgh to deal with it. Two semi-detached cottages have now been constructed on exactly the same footprint as the old buildings, and some of the original sandstone facings and coping stones were used to retain the character of the former buildings. The Bay Farm Cottages overlooking Munlochy Bay have proved extremely popular with visitors, who enjoy watching the seals sunning themselves on the sandbanks at low tide and the Ospreys occasionally catching a fish (see illustration 197). The disused Quarry beside Bay Farm had originally been used to provide stone for the construction of Fort George, an outstanding historic fortification near Ardersier, built in 1746 after the Battle of Culloden. The road through the trees to Bay Farm, past the Clootie Well of Craiguch and the old Quarry, was part of the Pilgrim's Way to St. Peter and St. Boniface Cathedral in Fortrose. This medieval church fell into disuse after the Reformation and is now a ruin, but the St. Boniface Fair is still held there in August each year.

In 2006, the decision was taken to renovate three more of the architecturally important buildings on the Estate, which had fallen into disrepair. The former Laundry (shown in illustration 104), a large two-storey building which had not been used for many years, and The Power House had both been designed by William Flockhart. The Power House had originally housed the generators to provide electricity for Rosehaugh House and this building, with its unique louvered ventilator, had survived the floodwater when the dam burst in 1946, though was now

derelict (see illustration 107). The other original building, which was in a very poor state of repair and urgently required preservation, was the former Boathouse (see illustrations 100 and 193). This unique oak-framed building with its pink pantile roof and first-floor balcony would not have survived many more years in its isolated position. A new road had to be made to the site so that the work could be undertaken for its renovation (see illustration 192).

All three buildings were extensively renovated and converted to provide first class holiday accommodation, which has proved very popular with visitors to the Estate, many of whom return to enjoy the peace of the beautiful surroundings. The former Powerhouse has been re-named Otter Lodge (see illustration 196) and the Laundry is now called Red Kite House (see illustration 194).

The permanent legacy of the Fletchers that remains here on the Black Isle does not lie in any ostentatious display of wealth, but is the result of the benevolent, wise and patient investment this family made in the land, the agriculture, the commerce and the livelihoods of the people of the area. The long view they took in these matters is what has helped to make this part of the Black Isle into the thriving community it is today and it is what will go on bearing fruit in the twenty-first century.

194. *The renovated laundry, now Red Kite House. Courtesy of Colin Heape.*

195. *The new Summerhouse on the ornamental lake. Courtesy of Stan Anderson.*

196. *The Power House, now Otter Lodge. Courtesy of Broadland Properties.*

197. *Bay Farm Cottages. Courtesy of Colin Heape.*

# Acknowledgements

WE acknowledge the financial assistance of Broadlands Properties in publishing the second edition of *Rosehaugh – a House of its Time*.

This second edition of the book comes twenty years after we brought out the first, and we have taken this opportunity to enlarge the format and incorporate some newly discovered photographs, making small amendments and additions where appropriate. We warmly remember the contribution of John Mills, former surveyor with Eagle Star, who started us off on the journey in 1996. We are grateful to John Shaw of Tordarroch who contributed many family photographs and not only wrote the Preface for our first edition, but was willing to advise on small changes necessary to the Preface of this edition.

We would like to thank: Maralyn Allan for all her work in re-typing the original material; Douglas Maclean who has made a huge contribution towards this new edition especially his skill in scanning original and new visual material; Russell Turner of Bassman Books for using his expertise to typeset and publish this new edition; Jack Hesling for providing wise and helpful advice throughout. We are particularly grateful to Colin Heape, factor of Rosehaugh Estate from 1996 to 2006, for his contribution to the final chapter both with a short update on the past twenty years and providing up-to-date photographs of the renovations done during that period.

We also gratefully acknowledge the advice and help given towards our first edition from The National Trust for Scotland and the late Brodie of Brodie who permitted us to use his mother's photographs from family albums in Brodie Castle.

Finally, we wish to thank the many people who, in contributing in different ways to the first edition, have made this second edition possible. The financial assistance of our original subscribers enabled us to publish the first edition and others were willing to share memories, anecdotes and photographs that enriched the content of the book. Any errors in reproducing such information are entirely ours and if any copyright has been infringed, we hope to be forgiven.

Hilda Hesling
Magdalene Maclean
Kathleen Macleman

Avoch Heritage Association
www.avoch.org

# Illustrations

35. The Hall: the fireplace.
36. The Hall showing clearly the Indian carpet.
37. The Small Ante Room. Courtesy of the Brodie of Brodie.
38. The Hall: c1900, showing the Indian carpet and a large tapestry to the left. Courtesy of the Brodie of Brodie.
39. The Drawing Room: a group relaxing.
40. The Drawing Room showing the furnishings.
41. The Drawing Room showing furnishings and the bay window.
42. The Drawing Room looking into the larger bay.
43. The Billiard Room: the walls in Moroccan leather. The doors into the Smoke Room.
44. The Drawing Room c1900. The young lady asleep in a Louis XV fauteuil (lot 674 in the 1954 sale). The fireplace can just be seen on the right. Courtesy of the Brodie of Brodie.
45. The bottom of the main stairs showing the corridor towards the Smoke Room.
46. The Smoke Room – panelled in cedar, with ormolu strapwork.
47. The Turkish Baths.
48. The Swimming Bath. All three photos courtesy of the Brodie of Brodie.
49. Roof window in the Swimming Pool and Baths area.
50. The Dining Room, the pair of doors into the Hall.
51. The Dining Room, west end showing fireplace and door leading to the corridor.
52. The Dining Room c1900. Courtesy of the Brodie of Brodie.
53. The Business Room: showing the built-in safe.
54. The Morning Room: c1900 showing the French kingwood writing desk (shown as lot 525 in 1954 sale). Courtesy of the Brodie of Brodie.
55. The Morning Room, south-west corner of the House, showing the fireplace and the fine plaster-work.
56. The Morning Room, the door onto the corridor.
57. The Morning Room Ceiling, style of Angelica Kaufman.
58. The Main Library, showing the imposing fireplace, probably installed later.
59. The first floor plan, William Flockhart c1899.
60. The top of the main staircase, showing the 21-light window.
61. The window in the Master Bedroom.
62. The Georgian bedroom c1900. Courtesy of the Brodie of Brodie.
63. The archway and steps leading to the Jacobean suite ('Elizabeth Room' on plan).
64. The 'Elizabeth Room': the oak canopy.
65. The Tower Smoke Room: the imposing stone fireplace.
66. The fireplace from the dressing room of the Georgian bedroom.
67. The Tower Smoke Room: the door to the stairs.

68. The door to the William and Mary bedroom (marked 'Jacobian' on plan).
69. Page 3 of the Catalogue for the 1954 Rosehaugh sale.
70. Louis XV Carved Walnut Fauteuil. Lot 674.
71. Chinese Porcelain Bowl. Lot 641.
72. The late Donald MacLeman in the presence of the Rosehaugh Buddha.
73. Japanese curiosities on the Terrace at Rosehaugh, 1902. Courtesy of the Brodie of Brodie.
74. One of the pair of Burmese Bronze chindits: September 1902. At the main entrance to Rosehaugh. Courtesy of the Brodie of Brodie.

*Chapter 8 – The Garden*

75. The garden staff of Rosehaugh c1910.
76. Section from G. Campbell Smith's estate map of 1850.
77. Garden plan by C.H.J. Smith, dated 1844. Courtesy of Mr A. MacArthur.
78. The gate towards the Slaughterhouse.
79. The Gardener's Cottage, built by Sir J.J.R. MacKenzie. c1850.
80. The garden wall and gate from the east.
81. Section of the Ordnance Survey map, first edition, 1871, Rosehaugh House and the gardens.
82. The Rosehaugh hothouses from the catalogue of MacKenzie and Moncur.
83. Section of the Ordnance Survey map, second edition, 1904, Rosehaugh House and the gardens.
84. Down the terrace steps.
85. A corner of the lower terraces.
86. The bottom of the terraces and the path to the lake. Courtesy of James Gow, Fortrose.
87. The garden pony, Rosehaugh c1900. Courtesy of the Brodie of Brodie.
88. Garden retaining wall showing drainage spouts.
89. The footbridge onto the island in the artificial lake. Courtesy of the Brodie of Brodie.
90. William Mortimer Moir, head gardener. Courtesy of Dr C. C. Moir.
91. The son and daughter of W.M. Moir, in front of Slaughterhouse Cottage. Courtesy of Dr C.C. Moir.
92. Willie Chisholm, last head gardener, viewing his plants.
93. Interior of one of the greenhouses showing the heating system.

*Chapter 9 – The Estate*

94. Rosehaugh estate map.

95. Middle section of The Dairy at Rosehaugh, used for making butter and cheese. Architect William Flockhart.
96. A complete view of The Dairy unit.
97. The Tower at the Stables.
98. The Horseshoe Falls.
99. The main lake. Courtesy of the Brodie of Brodie.
100. The Boathouse on the main lake.
101. Gray's Cottage, built c1900, William Flockhart, architect.
102. The Stables, with additions and alterations by Alexander Ross and William Flockhart.
103. West Lodge, Alexander Ross, architect.
104. The Laundry, William Flockhart, architect.
105. Kindeace, in Fortrose, originally the Estate Office, William Flockhart, architect.
106. The Smithy at the Mains Farm.
107. The Power House, William Flockhart, architect.
108. The workers' hut on Lime Walk.
109. The Summerhouse on the Ornamental Lake.
110. The Kennels Cottage.
111. The south side of the quadrangle at the Mains Farm built 1812. Courtesy of the Brodie of Brodie.
112. The Bothies to the east of the walled garden.
113. The Mains Farm, built 1884. Courtesy of K. MacLeman.
114. The Slaughterhouse and Cottage.

*Chapter 10 – The Domestic Scene*

115. Colonel Fitzroy Stephen CB of the Rifle Brigade, father of Lilian Fletcher. Courtesy of John Shaw of Tordarroch.
116. Lilian Stephen. Courtesy of John Shaw of Tordarroch.
117. James Douglas Fletcher wearing a monocle.
118. James Douglas Fletcher and Lilian Maud Augusta Fletcher in Ceylon. Courtesy of John Shaw of Tordarroch.
119. Lilian Maud Augusta Fletcher née Stephen. Courtesy of John Shaw of Tordarrach.
120. Violet Hope and Thomas, Rosehaugh 1900. Courtesy of the Brodie of Brodie.
121. Miss Lily Stephen in her pony cart. Courtesy of the Brodie of Brodie.
122. Violet Hope and her ponies, Lady Harriet and Rhona, Rosehaugh 1903. Courtesy of the Brodie of Brodie.
123. 'Seaforth in his motor' with James Douglas Fletcher. Courtesy of the Brodie of Brodie.
124. James Douglas and his niece, Lilian. Courtesy of John Shaw of Tordarroch.

125. Mrs Ethel Elford and her daughter Lilian. Courtesy of John Shaw of Tordarroch.
126. J.D. Fletcher relaxing in the main porch. Courtesy of the Brodie of Brodie.

*Chapter 11 – Public Service*

127. James Douglas Fletcher and John Henderson in front of the Estate Office in Fortrose.
128. Travels in Africa – 'Going into the drift' – Rhodesia, 1905. All photographs, courtesy of the Brodie of Brodie.
129. Travels in Africa – 'Coming out of the drift' – Rhodesia, 1905.
130. Travels in Africa – 'J.D.F. on the illimitable veldt, a thunderstorm coming on, and broken down.'
131. Travels in Africa – J.D.F. in Nubia, 1901.
132. The Clock Tower at Fortrose Academy,
133. James Douglas Fletcher at the Rosehaugh Estate, Eastern Transvaal, Africa. Courtesy of the Brodie of Brodie.
134. 'The Pride of the Highlands', Smithfield Champion, 1893.
135. King George V with Jock 1935. Courtesy of Royal Collection Trust © Her Majesty Queen Elizabeth II 2016.
136. 'Jock follows his Royal Master's Coffin', funeral of George V, 1936.

*Chapter 12 – Sporting Days*

137. Shooting luncheon at Rosehaugh. Courtesy of the Brodie of Brodie.
138. A hockey match showing J.D. Fletcher and Colonel Stephen, Rosehaugh, 1904. Courtesy of the Brodie of Brodie.
139. The same hockey match showing the Pavilion. Courtesy of the Brodie of Brodie.
140. James Douglas Fletcher and friends playing croquet. Courtesy of the Brodie of Brodie.
141. A game in progress on the curling pond above the boating lake.
142. Violet Hope at the presentation of a trophy in front of the Fletchers' bungalow on the golf course. Courtesy of the Brodie of Brodie.
143. Summer luncheon on the golf course, the Fletcher's bungalow at the sixth tee. Courtesy of the Brodie of Brodie.
144. Shooting luncheon at Auchterflow. Courtesy of the Brodie of Brodie.
145. Dinwoodie, the head game-keeper and his family at the Kennels Cottage. Courtesy of Mrs Stephen.
146. Page from the Game Book, 1900. Courtesy of the Brodie of Brodie.

# Bibliography, General Reading and Footnote references

## CHAPTER ONE

The best general reference book on the Black Isle is:
WILLIS, Douglas: The Black Isle, 1989
More detailed older sources include:
ORIGINES PAROCHIALES SCOTIAE, Vol 2. Part 2 1855.
OLD STATISTICAL ACCOUNT: Published between 1791 and 1799, this provides detailed descriptions of the parishes of Scotland. That on Avoch was written in 1793 by the Reverend James Smith. We have used the reprint done in 1981 and page references are to this edition.
NEW STATISTICAL ACCOUNT, 1845
THIRD STATISTICAL ACCOUNT, reprinted 1987.

Footnote references are to:
1. The Present State of Britain, no author, Part II, p113 onwards. Date: 1711.
2. Old Statistical Account, p312
3. Old Statistical Account, p323.

## CHAPTER TWO

Among numerous books on the MacKenzies are:
MACKENZIE, Alexander: History of the Clan MacKenzie, Inverness, 1879.
WARRAND, Duncan: Some MacKenzie Pedigrees, 1965.
BARTY, J.W: Ancient Deeds and other Writs in the MacKenzie-Wharncliffe Charter Chest 1906.
CLOUGH, Monica: paper on the MacKenzies of Scatwell for the Clan MacKenzie Society.

Footnote references are to:
4. Old Statistical Account, p304.
5. Old Statistical Account, p303
6, 7, 8 MacKenzie family papers.

## CHAPTER THREE

Information on the family came from:
MACINTOSH, Herbert: Elgin Past and Present, Elgin 1914.
Old Parish records of Elgin, and census returns from Elgin and Liverpool.
GORE'S Merchants' Directory of Liverpool.
Information on the alpaca trade:
JACOBSEN, Nils: Mirages of Transition: the Peruvian Altiplano, Univ. of California, 1993.
SIGSWORTH, Eric: Black Dyke Mills: Liverpool University Press, 1958.
HEWISON, G: Johnston's of Newmill, Elgin.

Footnote reference:
9. London Gazette: 12th October, 1855, vol 4, p3798.

## CHAPTER FOUR

Census records in Liverpool and Ross-shire, and the Records of Sasines Valuation rolls.
Information on agricultural improvements:
Transactions of the Highland and Agricultural Society of Scotland, vol 9, 4th Series, 1877.
Information on Alexander Ross:
BEATON, Elizabeth: Architectural Guide to Ross and Cromarty, RIAS, 1992.
MACLEMAN, Kathleen G.: Fitzroy C. Fletcher of Letham Grange and Ardmulchan, 2000.

## CHAPTER FIVE

There is now an excellent book on William Flockhart by Alan Calder, published in 2014 (see below), and there are references to his work in the following books, and we have also referred to biographical details, obituary notices etc. held in the RIBA file.

GRAY, Stuart: Edwardian Architecture, a biographical dictionary, Duckworth, 1985.
POWERS, Alan: Architectural History, vol 24, 1981: Architects I have known, the architectural career of S. D. Adshead, fragment of autobiography.
RICHARDSON, Margaret: Architects of the Arts and Crafts Movement, Trefoil, 1987.
SERVICE, Alastair: Edwardian Architecture and its origins, 1975.
BEATON, Elizabeth: Architectural Guide to Ross and Cromarty, RIAS, 1992.
Journal of the Royal Institute of British Architects, April, 1913.
The Builder, April 18th, 1913.
CALDER, Alan: William Flockhart: A Maverick Architect for the Nouveau Riches, 2014.

Footnote references:
10. Goodhart-Rendel: Roll-call in Alastair Service's Edwardian Architecture, 1975, p478.
11. Dawber, E Guy: Obituary, journal of RIBA, April, 1913, p449.

CHAPTER SIX

The quality of the drawings and plans of Rosehaugh reproduced by photogravure is not good, but can be found in the following:
ACADEMY ARCHITECTURE, vol 1, 1903, p70-73 and vol 2, 1904
BUILDING NEWS, Jan 1st 1904.
Adshead's account of the building of Rosehaugh can be found in:
POWERS, Alan: Architectural History (see ref. above in chapter five).

Footnote references:
12. Building News, Jan 1st. 1904.
13. Powers, Alan: Architectural History (see above).

CHAPTER SEVEN

The description of the interior and furnishings of the House come from accounts of visits to the house, photographic records, and the sale catalogues produced by Thomas Love & Son, Perth in 1954 and 1959.
For information on William Flockhart's designs for the Glasgow Exhibition:
THE CABINET-MAKER AND ART FURNISHER: July 2nd, 1888.
For information on the stained glass:
DONNELLY, Michael: Glasgow Stained Glass, Glasgow Museums and Art Galleries, 1981.

Footnote references:
14. The Baths Club: Rules, Regulations and Byelaws, 1894-95, p5.
15. Builders News, Jan 1, 1904.

CHAPTER EIGHT

General History:
REID, John: The Scots Gard'ner: first published in 1683, reprinted by Mainsteam, 1988, with an introduction by Annette Hope.
HALDANE, E: Scots Gardens in Old Times: 1200-1800, 1934.
DINGWALL, C, 1995, Researching historic gardens in Scotland, a guide to information sources; Scottish Natural Heritage Review no 54.

Footnote references:
16. Reid, John: The Scots Gard'ner, part 1 chap 1, p2.
17. Reid, John: as above, part 11, chap 2, p67.
18. Old Statistical Account, p303
19. Inverness Courier, Nov. 20th 1844.
20. Beaton, A.J.: Guide to Fortrose and the Vicinity, 1885, p38.
21. Inverness Scientific Society and Field Club, Transactions, 1893, vol 4 p269.
22. as above p 269.
23. Programme for the three day fête held at Rosehaugh, September 1903, to raise money for harbour improvements.

CHAPTER NINE

General Reference:
BUXBAUM, Tim: Scottish Garden Buildings, from Farm to Folly, 1989.

For information on the estate:
HENDERSON, John: articles printed in the People's Journal, July-August 1931.
ORDNANCE SURVEY MAPS: first edition (1871) and second edition (1904)
Recollections of many involved with the estate.

CHAPTERS TEN, ELEVEN and TWELVE

Information for these chapters on life at Rosehaugh has been provided by some of those who worked at Rosehaugh and their families.
We have also referred to:
FORTROSE AND ROSEMARKIE GOLF CLUB: Centenary booklet, 1988, by Alex Main.
SCARLETT, Meta: In the Glens where I was young, Siskin, 1988.
HOLM, Ena: The History of the Rosehaugh Stud, no date.
NOCK, O.S.: The Highland Railway, 1965.
BLACK ISLE FARMERS SOCIETY: A century and a half of the Black Isle Farmers 1836-1986, Douglas P. Willis.
Newspaper reports of contemporary events.
Ross-shire Directories.

CHAPTER THIRTEEN

ARTS COUNCIL OF GREAT BRITAIN: Lutyens Exhibition, 1981.

CHAPTERS FOURTEEN, FIFTEEN

Recollections and photographs from many people who attended the sales at Rosehaugh.
LOVE, Thomas & Son, Perth: Sale catalogues for:
1. August 1954 sale of furniture.
2. May 1959 sale of fittings.
Newspaper reports of the sales.

*198. Rosehaugh from the south, c1900, with James Douglas Fletcher on the path. Courtesy of the Brodie of Brodie.*

# Index

*James Douglas Fletcher, oil painting by David Alison. Courtesy of John Shaw of Tordarroch.*